ABBY ALDRICH ROCKEFELLER

THE MACMILLAN COMPANY
NEW YORK · BOSTON · CHICAGO · DALLAS
ATLANTA · SAN FRANCISCO

MACMILLAN AND CO., LIMITED
LONDON · BOMBAY · CALCUTTA · MADRAS
MELBOURNE

THE MACMILLAN COMPANY
OF CANADA, LIMITED
TORONTO

Abby Aldrich Rockefeller

BY

MARY ELLEN CHASE

THE MACMILLAN COMPANY

NEW YORK · 1950

*Printed in the United States of America
By The Haddon Craftsmen, Inc., Scranton, Pa.*

ACKNOWLEDGMENTS

IN THIS ATTEMPT TO PORTRAY AN AMERICAN WOMAN AND her contributions over a period of fifty years to our culture, I have received more assistance than it is possible for me to acknowledge. Over one hundred and fifty people have talked with me personally or have written me of their association with her, both as friends and as fellow-workers in the various interests and projects to which she gave so freely of her time and vitality. To list them all by name is obviously impossible. But I must especially thank the members of the Aldrich and the Rockefeller families, who have, on the one hand, been cooperative in every particular, and yet, on the other, have insisted on my complete freedom to write this book in my own way.

And I should be not only ungenerous, but dishonest, if I did not express grateful appreciation to two persons who from the beginning have given me immeasurable help: Margaret E. Burton, of New York City, who has selected the most pertinent documents from a vast amount of material, published and unpublished; and Dorothy Blair, of Abington, Connecticut, who has been my research assistant in the preparation and use of this material. Without them I could not have done this pleasant work of writing; and I cannot allow to pass unrecorded their constant help and interest.

MARY ELLEN CHASE

Smith College
February, 1950

FOREWORD

This book is the story of an American woman, whose generous years in terms of time were generously spent in terms of service. Singularly endowed with personal gifts of wit, charm, and gaiety, with a rare understanding and love of people, with keen intelligence and a quick sense of values, she lived her life with an intense and eager awareness of what life may mean when it is regarded as a loan and not as a mere possession. The pages which follow attempt to portray her as she quite simply was: the center and the security of a large family, brought up under circumstances requiring peculiar tact, humor, sanity, and wisdom; the patron of American culture in many forms; the constant friend of countless men and women; the disciple and the apostle of all things just and true, honest, lovely, and of good report.

CONTENTS

ILLUSTRATIONS

And what doth the Lord require of thee
but to do justly, and to love mercy, and to
walk humbly with thy God?

MICAH 6:8

ONE

TETLOWS AND ALDRICHES

1

W<small>HEN</small> <small>MISS</small> <small>ASENATH</small> <small>TETLOW</small>, <small>ON</small> <small>A</small> <small>MORNING</small> <small>IN</small> <small>THE</small> early 1880's, arose and began to dress, there was no more excited young woman in the city of Providence. She carefully arranged her auburn hair in a snood at her neck with braids across the top of her head and put on her black foulard, securing its neat white collar by a brooch of jet. Then she covered her shoulders with a black satin cape, took a last anxious glance in her mirror, and set out for the home of Senator Nelson Wilmarth Aldrich, there to begin her duties as governess to his several children.

Reared though she had been in a simple Quaker home, for her English parents were of that quiet persuasion, Asenath Tetlow could not have been unimpressed by the honorable career of her new employer and by the respect accorded him on every side. For Nelson Aldrich, coming to Providence at the age of seventeen from his father's Rhode Island farm, with but an education in the common schools and one year at East Greenwich Academy, had progressed with amazing rapidity from his original job as clerk in a firm of wholesale grocers, through various positions as a city official, to the Rhode Island Legislature. From there he had gone to Congress as a member of its House of Representatives, and finally in 1881, when he was hardly forty, he had won a seat in the United States Senate. Miss Tetlow surely knew him, as did everyone else in Providence, as an extremely popular and able public servant, almost entirely self-educated, deeply interested

3

in art, a lover of books and already the possessor of a fine library. The library must in itself have tempted Asenath, whose father and brother were schoolmasters and whose mother had early instilled in her a love of good reading.

The schoolroom which Miss Asenath entered on that memorable morning was at the top of the house at 565 Broad Street. She found it equipped with desks, blackboard and maps, and with an air-tight stove against wintry Rhode Island weather. She found awaiting her two little girls, a blue-eyed one of eleven named Lucy and a hazel-eyed one of seven named Abby, and two small boys, Ned and Stuart, whose still younger brothers were not as yet ready for her instruction. All her four charges proved to be lively youngsters, avid for fresh occupations and given not only to practical jokes but to friendly assaults now and then upon one another with their slates. They tested Miss Asenath's good nature as well as her ingenuity and made the Broad Street schoolroom anything but a dull center of learning and of life.

Miss Tetlow, true to the pedagogical theories and methods of her day, believed in precepts and in their frequent utterances. "To betray a confidence," she said to the young Aldriches, "is as grievous a sin as lying." "Think before you speak," she wrote on the blackboard, "ponder before you decide, consider before you act." She read a chapter from the Bible each morning and required the memorizing of many verses. She grounded boys and girls alike in American history, inculcated English grammar through diagraming and parsing, and taught arithmetic with such zeal that Abby at ten could proudly write to her "dear Dumpling Mama" in Washington that Miss Asenath had rewarded her efforts with 99 in that subject. The Tetlow manner of teaching spelling does not

4

seem to have been so successful, at least with Abby, who writes that her new mittens sent from Washington are "to big" and in the same letter asks for some "skats to go skateing." An echo of this blithe inefficiency, which she later ascribes to all Aldriches, persists, indeed, through-out her life in diaries and letters. Rubens to her clearly did not look odd as *Reubens*, and Rembrandt without his *d* easily retained his hold upon her affections.

Together with many more important disciples of her profession at that day, Asenath Tetlow looked with ad-miration, perhaps even with awe, upon German learning and straightway began the teaching of that language in the Aldrich schoolroom. The children each morning at the opening of school sang with her *Ein feste Burg;* and Abby's letters to her mother in Washington were now and again carefully signed: "Ich bin deine liebe Tochter." Apparently instruction in German to certain of the Provi-dence young was not relegated entirely to the Aldrich household, for Abby writes of a little boy of her acquaint-ance who replies politely in German to a question asked him in a horse-car! At all events, German was the foreign language taught at 565 Broad Street instead of French, which came later for all the children.

Miss Asenath's ministrations were not confined to the top story of the house on Broad Street or her horizon limited thereby. She frequently went to Washington with the family and during stays there, in the Arlington Hotel or in houses leased by the Senator from Rhode Island, continued her instruction in various improvised school-rooms. She accompanied a growing number of young Aldriches to the Capitol to observe with them affairs of State and to look with them upon important personages. She watched their behavior when they met their father's

friends, Senators Allison, Hale, and Frye, General Burn-
side, William McKinley, the engaging Mr. Thomas B.
Reed. And when she tied the sashes of Lucy and Abby,
preparatory to their brief appearance at their mother's tea-
parties, she gave them timely warning concerning their
manners when they should greet Miss Mary Lee, the
daughter of the great Confederate general, and Mrs.
Custer, the widow of that most famous fighter against the
western Indians.

With girls and boys alike she vastly enjoyed the privileges and sights of Washington, from the pictures in the
Corcoran Art Gallery, where she often took them, to the
thrilling appearance of Mr. Bancroft, the historian, who
often rode down Pennsylvania Avenue on his spotless
white horse. She went with them on excursions to Mt.
Vernon and to Arlington; and when they begged to go to
Alexandria, for the old church there was a favorite goal
of theirs, she marshalled them on a Potomac River boat,
since the road was often impassable because of Virginia
mud. In the evenings at home she accompanied Lucy and
Abby to the parlor, to greet their father and his friends,
who, over interrupted games of poker, were arguing the
burning political questions of the day. Just what might
the artful Mr. James G. Blaine be now devising for their
common hopes concerning tariff regulations? . . . Could
an income tax possibly be regarded as Constitutional?

And with all this cultural and intellectual fare, Miss
Asenath and the two Aldrich girls, according to some
Washington diaries of Abby's, went almost daily to Huyler's for a soda each, sometimes even two! Indeed, the
many references to Huyler's would suggest that its sodas
figured far more prominently, in Abby's imagination at
least, than the high matters of State on Capitol Hill. Nor

did they want for amusement and excitement at home where their colored cook, reputedly the best in Washington, not only performed culinary miracles but also could be relied upon for any number of dramatic scenes. She fought constantly with the butler and, when in danger of defeat, could use to perilous advantage knives, saucepans, and rolling pins. For some mysterious reason she wore her buttoned shoes on the wrong feet, the row of inside buttons always a matter of delighted conjecture on the part of the children. And, as a climax to her thrilling behavior, she allowed live terrapin to crawl at will about her basement headquarters!

2

By 1892, AFTER SENATOR ALDRICH HAD ACQUIRED THE gracious house with its trees and garden at 110 Benevolent Street in Providence, when Lucy had gone for two years to Farmington and Abby had entered Miss Abbott's School on Benefit Street for a year, and when the older boys were in high school, the sojourns in Washington became far less frequent for the family. Miss Fanny Tetlow now took over the care and teaching of the younger Aldriches, though her sister, Miss Asenath, still acted from time to time as companion and chaperone to Lucy and Abby. Both, indeed, wrought so effectually upon the minds and the imaginations of their pupils that even today their former charges "cannot remember life without a Tetlow."

Miss Fanny, whose hair like her sister's was long enough for her to sit upon, had a far sharper tongue than Miss Asenath and was not so easily influenced or trifled with.

She possessed, however, an extraordinary skill with anagrams, and, on frequent evenings, used this talent to good advantage in order to keep Abby out of the parlor where her sister Lucy was entertaining a succession of young gentlemen.

Not that Abby at seventeen lacked admirers of her own. Nevertheless, until after her graduation from Miss Abbott's in 1893 and her coming-out party in November of that year, her evenings were spent largely in studying her lessons except when she was rescued by the family for a game of whist or by Miss Fanny for anagrams. Boys in any number walked to and from school with her or from church, but the more formal entertaining of them was reluctantly sacrificed to Lucy.

At sixteen and seventeen she liked to read during the afternoon, either in the nearby Athenaeum or in "Papa's library." She read the stories of Sarah Orne Jewett, then at the height of her fame as a New England writer and a great favorite of Mrs. Aldrich, the novels of Charles Lever and those of Eugène Sue, Dickens, Jane Austen, Trollope, Dumas, George Eliot. She especially loved *The Marble Faun*. Sometimes, if she had finished her school work, she could read again at night; but frequent references in her brief diaries to hours spent with Shakespeare and Chaucer and with "compositions" about them, obviously requirements of Miss Abbott's establishment, would suggest that there were few such pleasant evenings. A large notebook, issued by Miss Abbott and entitled *Landmarks of History*, must in itself have occupied many hours, for it demanded complete lists of English and French "Sovereigns" with dates, parents, "consorts," "cause and place of death," and "important events of each

8

Abby Aldrich at Six

reign"; and this same exhaustive treatment was carefully accorded as well to each President of the United States.

She vastly enjoyed her coming-out party, an enjoyment prophetic of the future. All her life she "adored" parties and "the surprise of what different people do and say at them." "I confess, if I had my way," she wrote to one of her sons in later years, "I really think I should like to give a party every day." Her dress on that exciting afternoon, when she had just entered her nineteenth year, was of white satin trimmed with white tulle and white roses; and to her delight she received fifty-two bouquets. At the dinner following the party she sat next a young man named Mr. Frank Smith, who during the immediately succeeding years was to be much in evidence, and "had one of the best times I have ever had in all my life."

This gift of having a good time, this unquenchable gaiety and sense of fun, she never lost. Whether playing Old Maid or Authors as a child, on those rare Friday afternoons when "Miss Asenath let us out early for once," or riding on the cable car, or going down town with her friends for sodas, she always "had such fun as we never had before." She even enjoyed describing her moments of ill temper and exasperation. "Ned is such a baddest boy that I cannot possibly live with him." "Lucy makes me tired!" "I wanted awfully to go to the theater, but Mama would not let me, which I think was *Very* mean of her." "I went down street this afternoon with Lucy and Theodora. They both behaved very foolishly, indeed, and I was ashamed of them. This is one of the most disagreable days I ever saw. Albert Edward, the Duke of Clarence, died today." "Lucy has a five cent hat, trimmed with cheese-cloth. It is real prety, but it makes me look like a toad under a toad-stool."

9

Her mother thought her the most unpredictable of girls. "If I only knew beforehand what your sister Abby is likely to say or do," Mrs. Aldrich once remarked to Lucy, "life would be a lot simpler." For Abby had quite clearly not taken to heart Miss Asenath's early warning to "think before you speak, ponder before you decide, consider before you act." This quality of affording sudden surprise to her companions, however, may have done its share in attracting countless young men to Benevolent Street; for once the coming-out party was over and Abby had added her charms to the not inconsiderable ones of her sister Lucy, the boys who sought their hospitality and entertainment were legion.

Abby's engagement books and diaries for 1893 and the years following are little else than a roster of Providence young manhood. Charlie Merriman is staying for tea; Philip Mohun "looks perfectly sweet in his dress-suit"; young Dr. Peckham comes to call; Frank Thurston calls also, but alas! (for "he is very nice, indeed") on Lucy only. Harry Spooner takes her out sleighing, "a lovely ride"; Fred Hoppin "is awfully nice and good-looking, too," and she is happy over going to the theatre with him. Mr. Hoppin delights her further by asking her "to dance the German" with him, an invitation which she relays with some pride to Billy Dorrance when *he* tenders the same request a day too late. George Hinckley, Frank Thurston, and Dan George come in to play poker, and they all have "great fun until ten o'clock"; Wallace Howe invites her for lunch "at the Atheletic Club." She meets "several nice new boys at the Psi U. dance," all of whom have asked to call. Ed Barrows, Whitney Blake, and Royal Taft take her and Lucy to see the Republican Torchlight Parade, a most exciting occasion. Charlie Richmond gives

10

her any number of Providence sodas, which seemingly have retained their Washington charm; and she has "a perfectly glorious time at the Gym Ball," where she wears her new white muslin over blue silk, dances every dance and wishes there were twice the number, and has supper with Mr. James Coats, who brings her home at 2:00 A.M. A young man called Pug Guild is constantly bestowing his favors; and the ubiquitous Mr. Frank Smith continues with apparent success to steer his tenacious way among his rivals.

The number of Welsh rarebits which those young men, in quartets, sextets, octets, and even in hilarious groups of sixteen, cooked on chafing-dishes and consumed at 110 Benevolent Street on Sunday evenings leaves one astonished and incredulous. Sundays in Providence in the eighteen-nineties seemed incomplete and meaningless without this *pièce de résistance*. Rarebits fill the pages of Abby's diaries with amusing repetition; and each, whether concocted and eaten at home or enjoyed elsewhere, is likely to be "the best I have ever tasted in all my life."

Before the rarebits were made at the Benevolent Street parties, games were played, Truth and Consequences, Up Jenkins, Musical Chairs, Charades. After the rarebits, which were often dangerously complemented by cake and tea and by candy brought by the guests, there was much singing of old songs and popular favorites around the square piano. *Fair Harvard* invariably ended the party, regardless of the several college affiliations of the boys. Harvard was clearly Abby's first love, and she loyally inscribed her grief over any disaster that befell it.

Since Benevolent Street was in close proximity to Brown University, many young men found their way there from that campus, although in vacations Harvard, Yale, and

11

Princeton were generously represented. Football in the autumn and baseball in the spring, in Providence, Cambridge, and New Haven, and even as far afield as Williamstown and Hanover, meant gay weekends. Abby loved sports of all kinds, but only as an onlooker, never as a participant; and she once remarked to her sister Lucy that, were she called upon to dispense with any *one* possession, she should unquestionably choose to lose her feet!

Her feet, however, were actively engaged in fair weather; for walking with some young man on Sunday afternoon up and down the steep hills of Providence was an important social activity. Her engagement calendars record walks on practically every Sunday, often, though not always, with Mr. Frank Smith. Mr. Smith also frequently accompanied her home from her Tuesday afternoon drawing-class, although he yielded his place to others on the occasion of her Wednesday morning class in literature. Perhaps he cherished dreams of the future and was quite sensibly earning a living during the morning.

Senator and Mrs. Aldrich liked to have their home overflowing with young people. They were proud of their five sons and three daughters, a little girl named Elsie having completed the family circle. The Senator never outgrew an honest and even naive satisfaction in the pleasures which he was financially able to give his wife and children. He was frankly proud that his sons were intelligent and good-looking and that his daughters were handsome and charming; and both he and his wife had the rare gift of welding their family together in an easy and close companionship. According to Lucy Aldrich, who still lives in the old house on Benevolent Street, "there was nothing that Papa liked so much as to have Abby and me ask him for money for our one best dress each year, always providing we never chose brown, a color which he couldn't tolerate."

By 1895 he had purchased a piece of land on Warwick Neck on the shores of Narragansett Bay, a site which he had dreamed of for many years. There the family spent the summers in an old house so overflowing with themselves and guests that the one bathroom saw a good-natured line-up of a dozen or more waiting their turns each morning. It was not until some years later that the old house gave place to a new and larger one with the "modern conveniences" of another century.

It is impossible to overestimate the lasting influence which Nelson Aldrich had on his children. He was a man of many interests and enthusiasms; and he possessed in large measure the gift of instilling in others the resources, the satisfactions, and the values by which he lived. He took an eager delight in his new gardens, in trees and planting, in his farm and its animals, in sailing and in the pleasures it afforded him and his sons. An early, yet quite untutored, interest in art had urged him on to study paintings, which he was now able to buy and which never ceased to give him pride and excitement. His sons and daughters learned first from him those powers of evaluation and discrimination which were later to mean much, not only to themselves but to others. Almost never without a book in his hand and himself no poor literary critic, he taught his children by example rather than by precept that substantial world of good reading which was never to fail them. In 1894 he sent Lucy and Abby with Providence friends on their first trip to Europe; and in several following years he himself piloted them with their mother and a brother or two through the galleries of London and Paris, Munich, Florence, and Antwerp. He had a zest for

13

life and a frank enjoyment in what it could offer, whether in active physical pleasures or in the graces of the mind and the imagination; and this zest and enjoyment he communicated in full and generous measure to his children.

When Abby returned from Europe in the autumn of 1894, she was unable to say whether she had taken more delight in some Dover sole, which was her first dinner in England, or in the bag-pipers whom she had heard at a house-party in Ayrshire, or in the Yale-Oxford races on the Thames, or in her first sight of the Reynoldses and Gainsboroughs in the National Gallery, or in the Mediterranean at Mentone and Monte Carlo. Perhaps in the fact that all such "wonders" charmed her equally lay much of that awareness of life in all its aspects which she never for an hour lost.

TWO

YOUNG MR. ROCKEFELLER

1

In the spring of 1895, when abby aldrich is twenty-one, the name of a new young man occurs occasionally among the many who walk with her on Sunday afternoons or meet together at 110 Benevolent Street, that of Mr. John D. Rockefeller, Jr. At that time he was completing his second year at Brown University. Although he had gained admission to Yale after his preparation for college in New York at the Browning School on West 55th Street, he had chosen to enroll at Brown, partly because of its affiliation with the religious preference of his family, largely because its smaller student body made it seem more congenial and desirable than Yale to one of his nature and temperament.

He lived during his four years in Slater Hall, then the newest and most up-to-date dormitory on the campus; and, although he had to walk a quarter of a mile to the gymnasium for his bath, a general water-faucet in the hall, from which pitchers and basins were filled, and a small gas-stove in his otherwise unheated bedroom, spelled relative comfort, even luxury, for student life in the eighteen-nineties. The gas-stove provided also the means for evening chocolate-parties, which not only assured pleasurable conviviality and conversation at the time, but which were destined to play an important role in his later years. With a generous box of crackers, a five-pound can of Whitman's instantaneous chocolate, and a smaller one of Borden's Eagle Brand condensed milk on his cupboard shelf, he was equipped to act as host after study hours to various young men exhausted by Greek verbs and higher mathematics. His light housekeeping at Slater Hall bore testimony to his exact, careful, and well-ordered mind, for his cups and saucers were painstakingly washed in the hall after each repast and dried on dish-towels hemmed by himself. He was, in fact, no mean hand with a needle and thread, sewed on his own buttons and mended his own shirts; and he became early skillful, whenever circumstances required it, at pressing his trousers beneath his mattress. Sometimes he employed the further method of dampening their knees, laying them carefully on the floor, and placing upon them heavy music books, of which he had many.

Although he was an excellent student in the humanities and sciences, which at the close of the past century formed the rather narrowly prescribed college course, and distinguished himself by election to Phi Beta Kappa, he enjoyed also various extra-curricular activities. He sang a good baritone, was a member of the University Glee Club, and played the violin in the Mandolin Club. In his Junior year he was president of his class; in his Senior, he was manager of the varsity football team and at the end of the season showed a surplus in its accounts instead of the deficit under which for some time it had been uncomfortably functioning. He was deeply interested in church activities and in clubs for work among boys and men, although his native reticence made any public appearance painful for him. Indeed, the occasional necessity for a speech involved hours of embarrassed practice in his room, with himself reflected in the mirror as the sole audience of his slowly framed words.

Young Mr. Rockefeller had met Miss Aldrich at a dance during his Sophomore year and had been impressed not

only by her beauty and charm, but by her kindness—itself
an attribute of grace which at that period in his life meant
a great deal to him. For he was a shy and diffident boy,
who perhaps took a bit too seriously to heart St. Paul's
warning that one should not think more highly of oneself
than one ought to think. He had been brought up in a
deeply religious family under rigorous rules of what was
right and seemly in thought, pastimes, and behavior; and
he did not at first easily adapt himself to those gay social
events which seemed a necessary and inseparable part of
college life in Providence. Although he had learned to
dance as a small boy, he had never attended dances because his mother disapproved of such gatherings; and it
was not until his second year at college that he entered
upon the ordeal of taking further instruction in that art.
For many years thereafter he felt a lingering gratitude
to the "wall-flowers" at parties who not only greatly improved his dancing, but by their friendliness relieved his
embarrassment and made his early social paths, if not
those of extreme pleasantness, at least of relative peace.
He was neither ready nor easy at casual or light conversation; he was frankly, if unnecessarily, skeptical concerning any personal attractions which he might possess; and
his nature was not one to feel either elation or added self-
confidence because of a well-known family name and the
prospect of a more than considerable fortune. All in all,
he was a rather more serious and thoughtful young man
than many of those who happily claimed the hospitality
of 110 Benevolent Street; and, as time went on and he
became steadily more attracted to Abby Aldrich, he grew
increasingly doubtful of what he had to offer in competi-
tion with his numerous rivals there. Careful not to ask
her to dance with him until he could really dance well,

he nevertheless remembered her helpful graciousness to him and gained added confidence from it; and by the autumn of 1896, when she had returned from another summer in Europe, his name began to appear frequently upon her always crowded calendar.

Indeed, that summer of 1896 furthered his growing interest in no slight degree. With one of his sisters he himself went to Europe and from Hamburg made a cruise to the North Cape, Senator and Mrs. Aldrich, Lucy, and Abby being passengers on the same ship. In those days among the fiords and nights spent in watching the midnight sun, he and Abby dropped the formalities of Providence and took on for the first time the informality of Christian names. Graham crackers contributed to their ease and friendliness. He carried a supply of this prosaic sustenance in the left-hand pocket of his jacket, and Abby, who was often seized with sudden hunger, developed a way of impulsively helping herself from his pocket, a companionable gesture which gave him not a little conscious delight.

Once back in Providence and entered upon his last year in college, he began, perhaps unconsciously, to enlist her interest in those things which most deeply concerned him. For on her engagement calendar are clearly marked the many occasions upon which they attend church together. On practically every Sunday evening during that year they go to evening service. Mr. Frank Smith, still much in evidence, must have taken uneasy note of this particular engagement, for his name also begins to appear now and then as an escort to church, although in previous years he has not seemed to be religiously inclined! Young Mr. Rockefeller now frequently shares Sunday dinner with the Aldriches, or comes for tea; he also calls twice or thrice a week at Benevolent Street or invites Abby to go walking with him. She is his supper companion at the "Gym Ball"; he takes her to the theatre to see Julia Marlowe in *As You Like It*; at a musicale, given by his parents during a visit to Providence and followed by a dance, she is one of the most-favored guests.

As the spring of 1897 approaches and his final weeks of college hasten on toward Commencement, their activities increase in number and variety. They go together to baseball games, Harvard vs. Brown, Brown vs. Yale; they see an exhibit of Gibson girls, those models of grace and glamor to young women at the turn of the century; they attend the opera; they see a Wild West Show; on May and June afternoons they often ride a tandem bicycle; and on several exciting occasions they paddle up the Ten-Mile River and have their supper out-of-doors. On May 2nd of that memorable spring he accompanies her to the Beneficent Street Congregational Church, sees her accepted among its membership, and returns to dinner with the family; and on the Sunday following, she, being in New York, not only dines with his family but afterward enjoys with him several days of gaiety. In early June he goes with her on a day's jaunt to Warwick Neck to the Aldrich summer home, and, once his Commencement is over, he visits for five days there before returning to New York with his well-earned Bachelor of Arts degree and with, perhaps, some added self-assurance besides.

In the autumn, although she is still entertaining his rivals in Providence, she meets him during frequent trips to New York for shopping with her mother or for the theatre; and, although he is starting eagerly in business, he finds time for delightful hours with her. They see

Maude Adams in "The Little Minister"—an excitement
forever memorable to those who still recall it—and E. H.
Sothern in "The Lady of Lyons." They drive in Central
Park, go to concerts, and dine with his family. During the
next two years her New York visits increase in number
and manage to include, with him as companion, Richard
Mansfield in "Henry V," Maude Adams again, in
"L'Aiglon," and, for lighter fare, the incomparable Weber
and Fields. Nor does young Mr. Rockefeller fail to come
frequently to Providence where Miss Aldrich is now vary-
ing her social life by assiduously attending cooking-school
and art classes, becoming interested in the Providence
Y.W.C.A., a member, in fact, of its Board of Directors,
and occasionally taking over, for practice, the running of
the house on Benevolent Street. She is managing also to
find time for a great deal of reading which doubtless,
when the need arose, furnished material for conversation.
A list of books read in the summer of 1900 numbers twenty-
six and includes such diverse companions as Oliver Wen-
dell Holmes' *Autocrat of the Breakfast-Table*, Stevenson's
Kidnapped, three volumes of Bismarck's reflections and
reminiscences, Emily Brontë's *Wuthering Heights*, Mat-
thew Arnold's *Essays in Criticism*, and certain of the novels
of Mr. Henry James. And now on her calendar young Mr.
Rockefeller is no longer entered by his full name or even
by J.D.R., Jr. He has become merely John.

John was a deliberate as well as a reticent young man.
In any matter of judgment he was not inclined, after that
apt New England saying, to "swallow bait, bob, hook and
sinker" or to get hopelessly "entangled in the line." He
describes himself as even "a bit cold-blooded" about this
major decision of choosing a partner for life, since he had

22

been constantly pursued by the nightmare of making a fatally wrong choice and discovering it too late. His future entailed duties and obligations of which he was well aware; and his choice of a wife consequently meant to him searchings not only of heart but of head as well. He was still uneasily aware, during these problematical and indecisive years, of his Providence competitors, who had propinquity in their favor and who possessed, in his opinion, certain urbane and social assets which he could not claim. Nevertheless, from 1897 to 1901 he continued with quiet persistence his visits there, even while he realized that other suitors, less careful and cautious than he, were also running the race and but one obtaining the prize.

His sojourns at 110 Benevolent Street during these years, although they occurred as often as possible, were confined to a few brief hours. He went from New York on an afternoon train, dined and changed his clothes at the University Club, and presented himself in the evening, all too aware that by midnight he must be thinking of boarding the sleeper for his return home to work. Nor were the few hours always free from irritations and embarrassments, many of which centered about young Elsie Aldrich, who adored her sister Abby and was not eager to share with anyone else her attentions, especially if they seemed prophetic of the future. Elsie was extremely gifted at creating sudden necessities and desires which only Abby could supply or satisfy; and her peremptory and vocal demands from upstairs shattered the calm of many an evening. On one memorable occasion she descended in her nightgown with a Bible in her hand, summoned Abby into the front hall, and demanded as the price of her disappearance a sacred oath upon that Holy Book not only one of her sons, "that I didn't marry the man who asked me when I was eighteen, or even the later ones. I was nearly twenty-seven when your father and I were married; and I am sure I was better able at that age to judge the kind of man I really loved. Our greatest happiness has always lain in our perfect companionship, which has nothing to do with material things. I am happy and contented wherever your father happens to be. He always means home to me."

Young Mr. Rockefeller's several rivals rose nobly to news of the engagement, which was apparently communicated to them by Abby herself. Letters from six of them record their gratitude to her for writing to them personally of her happiness; and each of the six thanks her as well for her long friendship. One recalls her as a "little girl in starched pink cambric"; another announces gaily that, now he is "free," he regretfully supposes he "must look about for someone else"; all refer to what she has meant to them through the years; and he who had been most persistent and attentive of all says in closing that she has helped him more than she will ever know.

The Misses Tetlow also wrote of their unqualified delight. Fanny is confident that Mr. Rockefeller has chosen "the salt of the earth" and hopes only that he is "half as good" as his choice; Asenath is convinced that he is not only a fortunate, but a truly "splendid fellow"; and both are *sure* that he is to be congratulated, while they *really think* that such felicitous sentiments should be tendered their dear Abby as well; in short, neither Miss Tetlow feels a shred of regret or of apprehension except for the grief which her departure from home will cause her family.

And with the assured and complete delight of the elder

Rockefellers, whom Abby visited in September, the intense pleasure of John's three sisters, together with the approval of both families for an early marriage, few paths could have seemed more promising or free of obstacles.

3

THE GENIUS OF HIS FIANCÉE FOR ASTONISHING REMARKS and unpredictable behavior caused young Mr. Rockefeller, during the few weeks of their engagement, some amazed moments. "What you might say next, I never could tell," he wrote her a few years later, "but I always knew that I should probably like it better than what you had said last, however captivating that might have been."

With all his own generosity and interest in good causes he was more than a little surprised, not to say disappointed, over her immediate and summary disposal of an ample present of money, which, with much forethought and pleasure, he had decided to give her as a wedding gift. She might, he thought, like to buy something for herself from him, some work of art perhaps, something to signalize the occasion. Although he did not presume to ask what she had decided to do with his present, his natural curiosity suffered more than a slight shock when, a few days later, she informed him that she no longer had it.

"You see," she said, "I gave it away."

On another occasion, while she sat beside him in the Aldrich library, she suddenly announced that there was something which, she honestly felt, she must reveal to him.

"You may as well know it now as later," she said gravely.

With the uneasy remembrance of the many young men who had courted her before she had chosen him, young Mr. Rockefeller braced himself for a shattering blow.

Raising her hand from his, she detached from her front hair and dangled before his relieved and wondering eyes a small brown curl.

"It's false," she said.

4

THEY WERE MARRIED ON OCTOBER 9, 1901, AT THE ALDRICH home on Warwick Neck with her sister Lucy as her maid of honor and Elsie, at thirteen, now resigned to the inevitable, as her youngest bridesmaid. They went at once to Pocantico Hills near Tarrytown-on-the-Hudson to the home of the elder Rockefellers, who had relinquished it for their honeymoon. There for four happy weeks in perfect October weather they drove and walked in the quiet of the country, which they both loved, watching the sun set behind the Palisades, the lingering early morning mists in the valleys, which, she says in later years, always "fascinated" her. She loved to drive with him through the country roads and lanes; she loved the children in Pocantico Village, wild flowers, the autumn coloring in woods and thickets, the ducks in the ponds, migrating birds, the white frosts on late October mornings. "She was so gay and young and so in love with everything," her husband said long afterward, "that I kept wondering why she had ever consented to marry a man like me."

Perhaps, indeed, young Mr. Rockefeller was becoming aware, during the four weeks at Pocantico, of the elements of wonder and adventure latent in his marriage. For early in the honeymoon he was slightly stunned by his bride's definitive reception of excellent advice from him.

"I think it would be wise," he suggested, "if you formed the habit of keeping an expense account each week."

Her reply was as brief and final as it was instantaneous. "I won't!" she said.

Two days thereafter, before he had entirely recovered from this crisp shelving of one of his most ingrained and cherished notions, he was subjected on a pleasant afternoon walk to an equally sudden announcement, this time apropos of nothing at all.

"Do you know, John, that if you should ever strike me, I should leave you?"

The perturbed and bewildered husband of but a few days replied to this incredible ultimatum as one might expect.

"But, darling, I love you. I never would strike you. What an idea!"

"I don't suppose you ever would," she said, "I'm just warning you of what would happen if you ever *did*."

Needless to say, when the honeymoon was over and they went to New York to begin their life together under far less carefree circumstances, young Mr. Rockefeller had become abundantly convinced that, whatever life might hold for him, dullness and certainty would never be numbered among its offerings.

THREE

EARLY YEARS ON WEST 54TH STREET

ligious life of his family, become increasingly active in
church affairs, taught with signal success a Bible class
for men. His inherent modesty had not diminished with
the years, nor was it destined to do so, and now and again
it caused her good-humored irritation. "I really don't
think," she wrote to one of their sons, "that it is necessary
for your father to be quite so modest as he is." He had had
less time and inclination than she for those amenities of
social interchange among which Abby Aldrich had been
brought up and which she always loved. He now found
his somewhat circumscribed days suddenly infused with
an exuberance unfamiliar to him and with an enthusiasm for all the excitements and diversions of life, some of
which he would have been entirely willing to forego.

Perhaps, indeed, no two partners in marriage could have
been less innately similar than they. He was serious,
thoughtful, reserved, and inclined to be cautious and slow
in his judgments and decisions; she was gay, outgoing,
confident and quick in all her reactions. He was perhaps
over scrupulous in his adherence to moral and religious
precepts and principles; her spiritual nature, sensitive,
yet sure, was less disciplined than it was intuitive. He was
logical in his approach to most matters, seeing cause and
effect, thinking things through; she was often illogical.
Her imagination was more volatile than his, her humor
more ready, her fancy more rich. Although he had a keen
wit, a quick and apt sense of the comic, he was not, like
her, whimsical, delighting in fun for its very absurdity;
and he always took more pleasure in her merriment than
in those many diverse things which caused it: donkey rides,
"the most awful contraptions" on the heads of some brides-
maids, ill-chosen and unbecoming hats seen in church,
Donald Duck and Mickey Mouse, "Hellzapoppin", an old

The Broad Street Schoolroom

lady who, during a call, addressed her constantly as "Mrs. Roosevelt," the disgrace she felt from falling off a horse which suddenly turned to the right "and I didn't." He was precise and exact in his attention to particulars and details; she was likely to throw details to the winds, since she could go straight to the heart of a matter without them and, moreover, could gather them together later, disguised and more attractive than mere items. He preferred, whenever possible, to avoid large social groups, to shun casual and time-consuming conversation; she was in her element in the midst of many people and could elicit confidence and confidences from almost anyone.

"Your father is afraid that I shall become intimate with too many people," she wrote once when they were on a trip together, "and will want to talk to them, so generally we eat in what I call the old people's dining-room where he feels I am safer." And she hastily adds, with the justice always characteristic of her, that he has good reason for his concern since "my enthusiasm for all sorts of people is likely to carry me away."

"Your father gave me a lecture previous to my going to the dinner," she wrote again, "about my talking to Mr. Clark all the evening about the Museum, so I went very much chastened, but nevertheless with a small list concealed in my purse of things I really wanted to talk to him about."

Yet in spite of fundamental differences they possessed equally fundamental similarities. They shared a profound sense of the responsibility which one human being bears for the welfare of another and a genuine desire to fulfill that obligation; they respected the minds of others; they held tenaciously to what they believed to be right in human behavior; and although in many ways their cultural tastes were dissimilar and remained so, each cared deeply for whatever was best and highest in the nurture of the human spirit. They held in common a hatred of disloyalty in any form, toward a person or a principle, believing it to be of all offenses the most difficult to forgive. They never lost a consuming pride in each other. "I almost burst with pride," she wrote after thirty years of marriage, "as I sat behind your father while he made his speech. I hope some of you boys train your minds to the point where you are able to express yourselves so charmingly." "I am so proud of you," he writes her during an absence from home. "Your sweetness of character and disposition, your charm and your abilities make you the one woman in the world for me." And perhaps the strongest single tie which bound them together and was to be the primary and supreme influence upon them both was the sincere conviction that life is neither made nor judged by mere possessions.

2

POSSESSIONS, HOWEVER, WHATEVER ONE'S ATTITUDE TOWARD them, entail inescapable responsibilities. Although Abby Aldrich Rockefeller had been brought up in comfort, even in relative luxury so far as material resources were concerned, she was not accustomed to those details of management and supervision which confronted her upon her marriage. Moreover, she was married to a man who not only had been used to an extremely well-ordered home, but who admired orderliness and precision as indisputable values in themselves, who respected economy and care in the handling of money, and who regarded himself, first of all, as the steward of a vast and ever-increasing fortune, the wise employment of which was both his moral obligation and a matter of personal honor. For the fulfillment of his ideals he expected and relied upon the cooperation of his wife in action as well as in outlook. He received both from the beginning.

The house at 10 West 54th Street, of which she early became both mistress and manager, demanded a supervision quite undreamed of by that virtuous woman in Proverbs who "looked well after the ways of her household." One of the largest private residences in New York, it had been designed and built not only for a growing family and frequent guests, but for necessary public engagements and entertainments. Its nine stories included an open-air roof playground, a gymnasium and an infirmary for the children, family bedrooms, guest suites, comfortable living and working quarters for a large staff of servants, and on the lower floors a drawing-room, library, and music-room. Its very size and its constant activities demanded a care and a competence which Abby Aldrich Rockefeller was never willing to leave to others. She knew her kitchen and her storeroom, her linen closet and her china cupboards. If a luncheon for seventy-five guests was in order, she decided upon the food and took note of its cost; and although she never overcame her early aversion to personal expense accounts and once laughingly remarked that her financial adviser "nearly had a fit" because she had almost given away "more money than I really have," she shared her husband's aversion to display of any sort and always avoided unnecessary or lavish spending.

In addition to the house in New York she had to keep

35

a watchful eye on the one at Pocantico Hills where they spent many weeks throughout the year and on that at Seal Harbor in Maine where they spent much of the summer. Housekeepers, however able, rarely found themselves left to their own judgments and decisions. She was always on hand for early morning conferences with them, discussions about the food for the day, the discreet darning of curtains which "could be made to do for several more years," the re-upholstering of chairs or sofas ("Is it really necessary? I don't mind a bit of clean dust myself."), the purchase of new linen during the January white sales. "At the present moment," she once wrote her sister Lucy, "we have four houses open, all more or less needing my attention, and I must say I have my hands full."

She had a genius for living comfortably with her many servants, for making them feel that they worked with her rather than for her. She knew their backgrounds and personal problems and was a friend to all of them. She knew that one had a hobby for moving-pictures and had him bring in his projector and screen so that she might enjoy them; she was anxious over another who was ill and who might be unhappy and discouraged in a hospital; she loved to talk with George who skillfully mended her Oriental rugs, and she let him know that she admired the work of his hands and shared with him a feeling for old design and color; at Pocantico Hills she taught the Italian gardener, Carmine, once a tailor and at first unused to flowers, how to grow them, even how to arrange them.

She took care that the members of her staff had a change of scene, planning shifts for them from one house to another. When social engagements were especially heavy, she would say to her New York housekeeper over her breakfast, "Come in and laugh with me before we get started on this day. It's going to take some laughing to get through." She once wrote of her relief that she herself tipped over a glass of water after the embarrassed butler had spilled some coffee on her dress. "I think it consoled him that I had upset things, too."

All of them testify to her constant good humor, her quick understanding, the sense of friendliness she always gave them. "She could be outspoken, even downright, when she told us what was wrong with our work, but she always did it in such a way that we wanted to make things right." "She used to show us her new dresses, ask us what we thought of them, and which one she would look best in." "She had a way of waving her hand to us as she left the house which somehow made us feel good, and she never forgot to do it." "She taught me to love beautiful things, flowers and china and the way the table was set; and after the guests were gone, she was always hurt if no one had mentioned how nice things had looked or how beautiful the flowers were. 'Just think, Eini,' she would say, 'no one said a single word about all our work.' "

3

"THIS MORNING WHEN I REMEMBERED THAT IT WAS MOTHer's Day," her son Winthrop wrote her when he was eighteen, "I tried hard to think just why there was a Mother's Day. It seemed strange to me that anyone would need to have any particular day set aside in which to remember his mother, but then the question answered itself. Everybody couldn't have a mother like you."

Young Winthrop Rockefeller's appreciation of his mother is but one of many in the letters of her children, and the perennial source of that appreciation lies on every page of her countless letters to them from their childhood on. To her from the beginnning the quality and the character of her home were first and foremost. Her family and its welfare demanded and received her vitality, her wisdom, and her common sense. She was, indeed, its "center and security." Her constant thought, care, and work for it, her concern for the individual mind of each of her children, was, moreover, encouraged and enlarged by the vision which she cherished of the American home at its best. For she saw it quite simply as the foundation of American culture and democracy, the strength and the sanity of coming generations, in short, the chief hope of our civilization; and to it she devoted all that she had within her.

In the twelve years from 1903 to 1915 her six children were born, a daughter and five sons. She realized from the start, as did their father, that their upbringing and training would require especial tact and wisdom because of their inescapable position in society. "I am happy to know that you were generous with the money I gave you," she wrote a twelve-year-old son, "and that you made other people happy with it. Money is wonderful to have when people do good things with it; but it is very dangerous to have if people do selfish, bad things with it." She disliked publicity of any kind and took every care to avoid it for the children. She wanted above everything else to instill within them values which had nothing to do with material possessions; and to this end she planned and shared with them their occupations and amusements.

Once they were old enough, each took part, turn by
38

turn, in family prayers, which were held before breakfast. She copied Bible verses on bits of cardboard which, she believed, would make the memorizing of them more welcome. She agreed with their father that family prayers afforded a good opportunity to air the personal grievances among them, to discover together where justice lay and who had been hasty or unkind.

She saw them off to school, and in the late afternoon she was always at home when they returned. No meeting, however important, no social engagement, however pleasant, was allowed to encroach upon five o'clock or to extend for her beyond that hour. From five to six she was with them, either reading aloud to them or listening as one or another read to her whatever he especially liked. Her letters to them on the infrequent occasions when she had to be away refer again and again to their books. "I am glad that you like *The Wind in the Willows*. Of course, I knew you would. What are you going to read next?" "I hope that you will find time to finish *Vanity Fair*, for it will well repay you." "I think the poem you copied for me is very beautiful. I hope you will memorize lots of good poetry because, as you grow older, you will find that it will give you great pleasure."

In the evening, after their early supper, she often supervised their study, hearing Nelson say his multiplication tables, worried that he did not know them better. She sometimes copied out and corrected the misspelled words in their letters to her, although she frankly admitted to them that she had to consult the dictionary often and feared that they, like her, had all inherited "the Aldrich inability to spell."

Her letters to them while they were still young children constantly reflected her own interest in things about her and encouraged them in an early knowledge of birds, trees, and flowers. "I bought you a little magnifying glass yesterday, and I am sending it to you. You can look at flowers and bugs and all sorts of things through it." "There are so many jays here in Florida that the air is filled with cries of *thief*, *thief*, *thief*. They are beautiful birds to look at, but their table manners are very bad. For the last three days a pair of cardinals have been here, and they are much the prettiest and gentlest of all the birds. We are looking now for the coming of the cedar wax-wings." "Everywhere here in Maine the leaves are beginning to turn. I wish you could see the exquisite colors which the blueberry and huckleberry bushes make under the trees." "I can hardly wait to have you come home, for we can have such great fun together studying the birds and insects."

In spite of her personal dislike of expense accounts, she kept a careful eye upon those required of them. "Don't forget to keep your accounts. Papa will want to examine them." "I am glad you have saved twelve dollars for your Christmas presents. I will go shopping with you, and, if we are careful, I am sure we can make it do." When Winthrop at boarding-school took time from his studies to earn money by cutting the hair of forty of his schoolmates, she wrote him that she feared this was "poor economy in the end."

She loved giving children's parties perhaps because of the problems inherent in them and the inevitable brief disasters.

"The party yesterday came near to peril at several moments. The two Douglas boys sulked and refused to play because they thought Find the Thimble too childish. The older one said he preferred Chess! The younger Fosdick cried because she got beaten so often at all the games, and

40

I am sorry to say that David pulled the hair of the other. Nelson and Winthrop had a short, but most intense fight. It was all great fun, though I was so exhausted at the end of it that I could do nothing but go to bed. John was busy at his desk and wisely kept out of the way. Their table manners left much to be desired and I fear would have shocked him."

She encouraged the children to have pets and to care for them, and the tragedies which were forever occurring always drew her sympathy. "I'm terribly sorry over the death of your mother rabbit. Do you suppose she could have died from eating your shoe-strings?" "We had a sad event in the house last week. One of Nelson's fish died. He got three new ones and put them in the bowl with the three old ones and one pollywog. Perhaps there were too many in the bowl. Anyway one of the old ones got a crack in his tail and two days later he died." "The police puppy that we have bought you is due to arrive tomorrow morning. I hope he doesn't come until we get there, poor little thing. He will be used up after travelling so long, and we must all be especially kind to him."

She reminded them of consideration for others, attention to old people, sympathy for those who were lonely or shy. "Old people like to be made a part of things. Don't forget to go out of your way to make them feel wanted and at home." After she had taken one of her sons to boarding-school for his first year, she wrote to him about a boy whom she had noticed standing by himself on the playground and apparently lonely and ill-at-ease. "I hope you will take pains to get acquainted with him right away. I hate to think of him homesick and sad." "I'm distressed oven Ben's flunking his exam. Wouldn't it help him some if you brought him home when you come this weekend?

41

We could take him to a play to cheer him up. I could pay his fare if you think that would be wise and not embarrass him."

Even while the children were still young, she respected them as individuals and never "talked down" to them. As far as possible, she gave them the responsibility of making their own decisions. She rarely told them her plans for them, but rather asked them for ideas and advice. Whether her oldest son was choosing the material for new curtains in his room or her youngest was deciding how he could best spend the dollar he had saved, the problem, as well as the consequences, was his alone. When her daughter began to smoke, she was allowed to choose between that indulgence and an increase in her allowance. On her son Winthrop's seventeenth birthday she wrote him that, since she considered him "really grown-up now," she would appreciate it if he would take over the plans for a proposed party and run it himself. "My only stipulation," she concludes, "is that, if you ask an extra girl, she shall be nice-looking." If Winthrop and Laurance think it will be more fun to come home from camp alone rather than in her company, "my feelings will not be hurt in the least. Be quite frank with me about it." "Loyalty and gratitude seem to be rather rare virtues, and it is a satisfaction to me whenever you children show appreciation for what is done for you or when you are especially loyal to your friends, even if I don't happen to admire the friends you are loyal to."

Just as she never hesitated to tell them plainly what had displeased or disappointed her in them, she never forgot to thank them for generous acts or to commend them when they deserved praise. When she went to China in 1921, "because I cannot let your father go alone," her dearest possession on the long journey was a little pillow which her six-year-old son David had made for her. "Everywhere I go, your balsam pillow goes with me." She was sad when the lady's slippers which Laurance gathered for her arrived in bad shape, but she cannot thank him enough for his thought of her. Both she and his father were delighted that he had learned to manage a horse so gently and skillfully. She was immensely proud when Nelson and Laurance, in Labrador one summer on a Grenfell schooner, proved that they could cook for the crew, even though they did it so well that they had to remain in the galley even after the sick cook got well.

"As I look into the future," she wrote in 1922 when the oldest of her six children was nineteen and the youngest, seven, "I see that we shall not have a very quiet or peaceful life for many years to come. Still I am never completely happy, even with all the confusion, unless we are all together under one roof." And under that one roof, with all the differences in age and personality, she managed to weld her family together by enlisting the understanding and the generosity of each toward the others. She explained in confidence, even in fun, to one child the idiosyncrasies of another, for the moment setting aside his own sometimes irritating traits.

"I hope, when you boys come home, you will do nothing to disturb David's present friendly feelings with Winthrop. It seems cruel to me that you big boys should make Winthrop the goat all the time. I realize that he is often trying, but you know very well that the only way to help him is by being kind to him. Abuse only makes him angry and much worse, while for love and kind treatment he will do anything. Also, remember how young David is, take time to play with him, and be good to him."

43

In a speech given in May, 1927, before the Cosmopolitan Club of New York on the subject of the American home as the basis of our civilization, she stressed the necessity for "confidence, freedom, and cooperation" between parents, without which they are "soon on the road to boredom, disillusionment, friction, and disaster." She deplored the "general and sentimental assumption that the mother is alone, or even pre-eminently, the center of the family." The young Rockefeller children were allowed no such misconception. They were instead made aware of their mother's reliance upon their father and of her pride in him. She wrote them of his pleasure in their letters home, of his hopes and desires for them, warned them against behavior which might worry or displease him. "Your father is so modest, so unassuming, and often so doubtful of his own ability that I wonder if you always realize what a tower of strength he is to me and to us all." "I really feel sorry for the unhappy people who cannot find in their married lives the companionship which your father and I have always had." And in one letter she humorously bunched all the family into one unsatisfactory group in contrast to its head: "Your father is so wonderfully thoughtful himself and so considerate of all the people with whom he comes in contact that I am sure he must occasionally find the rest of us somewhat difficult. Perhaps there is a little bit too much Aldrich in us and not enough Rockefeller!"

When the "many years" to which she referred with philosophic anxiety were over and the children were in college or in business, she once received a letter in praise of the success with which they had been brought up. Her reply was characteristic:

44

"John and I have gotten to the point where we feel that perhaps the children have brought *us* up. So if, as you kindly suggest, they are a success, I really think we must give them the credit."

4

IT WAS LUCKY THAT ABBY ALDRICH ROCKEFELLER "ADORED parties." From the beginning of her marriage she was either hostess or guest at a number sufficient to quench the most vivacious of spirits. Not only did she encourage the children to invite their friends for meals at any time ("David insists that every teacher he has ever had at the Lincoln School must come to supper.") and entertain innumerable business or philanthropic associates of her husband, but she was constantly acting as hostess to public gatherings of one sort or another, various boards of the Young Women's Christian Association, with which she early became connected, church groups, others interested in art, or education, or work among minority races, particularly the Negroes. A description of a typical week in her life is given in a letter to one of her sons:

I am going to Philadelphia tomorrow to see the Persian exhibit, and Commander Byrd is coming to tea so I must be back at five o'clock. Tuesday the Batchelders are coming to visit us for three days, and Tuesday evening Dr. Breasted is giving a lecture here to about a hundred people. He will stay here, too. Wednesday we are all dining out, and on Thursday we are giving a big party. On Friday you come—how glad we shall be to see you and that day is yours!—but on Saturday evening we must again have dinner away from home.

Her quick judgments of people and the amusement they afforded her kept her from weariness or boredom. "Mrs. D.P.H., who is seventy-five, monopolized all the attention and conversation. I longed to tell her that in all those years she should have acquired more tact." "I have never seen anyone eat quite so much as Mr. F. did." "We played some feeble bridge after dinner which everyone politely pretended to enjoy." "Neither her dress nor her bag seemed to have any relation to her hat or to each other." "I like her and think her a most amazing person, but thank the Lord I don't have to live with her. I don't wonder her husband looks slightly crushed." "He looked to me like one of those French titles who take care to marry a rich American girl." "I could not get up a great enthusiasm for Mr. A's new wife, probably because he is her fourth husband. Your father thinks that is being a little fussy on my part."

Then, too, there were always compensations for even the most tiring of evenings once their guests had gone or they had returned home. Sometimes they practiced a few of the new dance steps; often they read aloud for an hour or turned on the victrola and listened to music, which they both enjoyed, before they went to sleep. And frequently her husband's college enthusiasm for hot chocolate was renewed late at night on West 54th Street. "I forgot the dullness of the party once we had got home, for your father treated me to a cup of delicious chocolate in his dressing-room, and we had such a happy time together. I feel sorry for all the women in the world who haven't as good husbands as I have."

Even her dislikes kept her from being bored. They were many, and she did not hesitate to express them. She hated certain magazines and certain "terrible" news commentators, the latest kind of musical revues, "which your father and I clearly do not understand," Gothic architecture "when it is obviously out of keeping with time and place," badly mannered or pretentious people, "flattering and fawning." She hated to eat in restaurants. "I am frightfully suspicious of the dishes. I'm perfectly sure that those small places which you children enjoy so much have not proper facilities for sterilizing dishes." She preferred "slightly worldly ministers" and was annoyed by "heavy-hearted ones." She hated voluble piety or unctuousness, personal publicity, race prejudice, crows, "chairs made for lounge-lizards," and bad taste in dress.

Her own love of clothes lent a spur to her public appearances or, for that matter, to those only among her family. "She would stand for half an hour before the mirror," her husband said, "once a new dress or hat had arrived, fixing this or that, and she would be hurt if I didn't leave everything to see how she looked. 'I don't believe you like it,' she would say. 'You haven't half looked at it. Put those stupid papers down and pay a little attention to your wife.'" She loved all shades of blue and green and was especially partial to gray, although sometimes she made daring excursions into brighter colors. "I have a new bright purple dress to go with a new hat. I fear the whole is perhaps too dressy, but I think your father will enjoy it." She took especial care "to look just right" when the children came home from school "so they won't think their mother is slipping."

Hats were her greatest dissipation, and she never could resist them. "I have a new hat with lilies of the valley on it. It is very silly, but it does cheer me up; in fact, nothing gives me such a lift as a new hat." She loved flowers and other gay ornaments on them and cherished any compliments she received about them. "Everyone at the Board Meeting liked my hat, though I think they were a bit startled at first by the odd fruit on it. I told them it was meant to suggest a Harvest Home Supper." She was delighted to receive a letter from the president of a college, who said that, although Mrs. Rockefeller's speech had been excellent, the thing that had intrigued her far more than the speech had been "that charming hat" which she had worn. "I have a new hope for education," Mrs. Rockefeller wrote in describing her pleasure in the letter, "when the president of a woman's college is not blind to hats. As a matter of fact, she had on an encouraging one herself." She always wore her gayest hats to church "to cheer people up." And once, when she was dreading a conference at which she feared unpleasant altercation, she sent a hurried note to a friend. "Have you a really wild hat that I might borrow for the afternoon? Mine are all too tame, and I want something to amuse those worried women."

The many social affairs which she herself gave were always enlivened for her by the things she used at them, her china, linen, and silver, which she frankly loved. She was quick to see the personality latent in inanimate objects. "I never knew a person who loved to touch things as mother did," one of her sons said. "She could somehow make anything come to life just by putting her hands on it." The past in certain of her possessions always appealed to her. "I'm always wondering about all the hands that have held these old cups," she would say, "all the things that were in the minds of those who owned them years ago before they came to me."

5

AN INTERESTING EXCHANGE OF LETTERS WAS PUBLISHED IN *The Atlantic Monthly* in 1919 and 1920, the first letter written by a neighbor of the Rockefeller family, the reply to it by Abby Aldrich Rockefeller.[1] They are given here because they show the perhaps natural attitude toward great wealth and the misunderstandings and barriers which are often its result.

WRITTEN, BUT NEVER SENT,
TO A VERY RICH NEIGHBOR.

My dear Mr. Aristos,—

Since you moved into this neighborhood and bought a thousand acres of land, we have lived within five hundred feet of one another for seven years. Your lady and I exchange calls and have long pleasant chats. Our children lunch together at each other's houses; we accept each other's invitations to dinner, and I think we all four enjoy these occasions. The boys and girls exchange proffers of outdoor sports to be enjoyed together; though yours seldom accept because they are too busy with lessons, and so ours are sparing of their own acceptances.

Certain privileges of wood and water which we enjoyed before you created your estate, we continue to enjoy with your courteous encouragement and apparently to your entire satisfaction. You also offer to sell us vegetables at low rates, or to give us kindling from the enormous piles of packing-boxes which accumulate in your back premises from time to time; and you do various other little acts, trying to help make life agreeable for us.

[1] These letters are reprinted by permission of *The Atlantic Monthly*.

When we asked you to sell us a parcel of land—sixty by seventy feet—which we had not been able to secure from the former owner, in order to complete our precious three acres, you offered us the free use of that bit 'just as if it were ours, without payment' saying that you disliked ever to part with any land.

When we heard you were coming near us, we were troubled, for we feared the close neighborhood of elaborateness and formality and pride. We were afraid our children might have to learn that there is arrogance even in America. But not so. You are simple. You are kind. You have been in every way a good neighbor, a remarkably good neighbor.

It is curious that, after seven years of such perfectly friendly intercourse, we are not friends. We know a great deal more about each other than we did in the beginning; but we do not really know each other any better at all. This is the more odd, because we have so many points of agreement in matters which make the most difference between folks. A sense of duty is the leading emotion in your lives as well as in ours. You are sincere; you, too, are interested in social betterment, and in educational improvement; you like the same sports. We all four enjoy the same magazines (the *Atlantic* being the sole reading of any one of us sometimes for weeks), and we admire the same public men. Your land is just like ours, only there is more of it. Your house has the same appointments as ours, only there are more of them and they are finer. We all wear the same kind of clothes, only you have more of them. Each couple loves its own children more than anything else except, of course, each other. We all admire and cultivate the same kind of manners; we even enjoy the same kind of jokes. What more is necessary to make people friends?

And yet, we are not friends. As I see it, the explanation is *your money*,—your extra money,—not the money you spend, but the money you have not spent.

We are so afraid that you will think we are after it, that we dare not talk freely on any of the subjects which interest us most deeply—because those subjects are all *objects;* and *objects* always need money. You are so redundantly rich! Whatever one of our dreams we might begin to be eloquent about, we could not long conceal the fact that it was still but a little way toward fulfillment—for lack of money. In short, whatever we said, we should consciously fear that we sounded like beggars. And beggars, satellites, or dependents, we will not be. We have a fixed determination not to ask money for any of our projects from people who are not already eager to give.

And on your side, we are utterly at a loss to know how you feel. We have an impression that we do not seem to you of the slightest importance. Your refusing to sell the strip of land to us seemed to us equivalent to saying, 'We do not care to make you at home near us. We think of you as of birds who have nested close by. We treat you with consideration, and we watch you with interest, but we shall not care when you flit, leaving the nest empty and ourselves more free to range at pleasure beneath your trees.'

Nothing you ever say or do seems to prove anything different. There is, indeed, a possibility that you are as diffident as we. Perhaps you like us as fully as we like you, but are afraid that we do not find you interesting. But no! A rich man practically always looks upon a man who has not made money as a failure, unless he has gained fame. Even then, he inclines to doubt the value of a fame which cannot gain financial recognition. As a matter of fact, are you not all the while silently on the watch to avoid encroachments from us, and to elude possible openings for favors to be asked? Are you not all the time on guard against our becoming beggars, satellites, or dependents?

And so it goes; we take the privileges of wood and water, because we believe that in a properly conducted state these

51

opportunities would be ours of public right. We do not take other favors which you offer, because we believe that in a properly conducted state those things would still be matters of private right, and we have no special claim upon you. We have not the claim of friendship, which is the only basis upon which one can accept private favors. In a friendship, the exchange of invisible benefits is so great, so constant, and so valuable, that tangible benefits are given and received without consideration of money value, simply as outward expressions of that inner interchange.

Do you remember that, several years ago, after we had once or twice invited your boys to go sailing or snow-shoeing with us, you offered to employ my husband to take charge of their sports all the time? So it goes. You look upon us as a duty, and as a possible convenience, but never, it seems to us, as possible friends. We are sorry, for we like you candidly, and you are our nearest neighbors.

Yours cordially,

Your Friend and Neighbor.

P.S. I cannot send you this letter, because you might think it sheer impudence; or, if you did not, any efforts which you made thereafter to become friends would seem to us to spring from your all-pervasive sense of duty, and we should give them a cold reception as being favors which we had asked for. We will not be beggars.

To the Editor of the Atlantic Monthly.

It is seldom that an unsent letter reaches its destination. As this one was received through your columns, may it not be answered in the same way? For your information, may I say that I am the wife of the "Very Rich Neighbor."

My dear Neighbor:

I agree with you that we are not intimate friends, though friends I had felt we were. I do not agree with you, however, as to the cause.

Your "Rich Neighbor" gives ten months of the year unreservedly to the task of administering his stewardship to the end that the wealth entrusted to his care may bring enlarged opportunity, health, happiness and comfort to his fellow men. His wife is his ardent supporter and feeble imitator.

The two months which he spends as your neighbor give him his only opportunity to play. During this time his aim is to become intimate with his children, to read the books he longs to read, to exercise out of doors, to get near to Nature, to have time to think, to meditate, to plan; in other words, to refresh his spirit. At such a time it is not that one does not want to see one's friends; it is simply that to be worth while to one's friends and the cause of righteousness, one must—so to speak—retire into the wilderness. Moreover, during this vacation there are duties which interfere with a greater interchange of social visits, such as an enormous mail which persists in coming and must be answered. Under the circumstances, the mere fact that your "Rich Neighbor" prefers to spend his mornings chopping wood or riding and playing tennis with his boys, his afternoons driving or walking—he and I together—his evenings with the children, inevitably results in but little time remaining. It may seem selfish, but it has nothing to do with money.

Admiring your husband immensely, we sought for our boys his companionship. To offer compensation for his added responsibility seemed only fair.

Why my husband did not sell you the strip of land, I do not remember. I suspect, being mere man, he simply didn't want to. It was entirely impersonal.

Most rich people seem unresponsive, but it is not entirely their fault; they are not treated naturally. My husband and I were once asked to a simple home where I know they had delicious baked beans; we were treated to poor roast chicken. The rich are given what they are expected to want, both intellectually and gastronomically. It may be flattering but it is not stimulating or wholesome. A sense of humor and a good mind may be hidden beneath a tiara.

To their faces the rich are often accorded a respect that is not felt, and behind their backs a contempt that is not deserved.

Please, dear neighbor and dear reader, too, help the deserving rich by not taking us too seriously and by forgetting that surplus money.

Sincerely,
Mrs. "Aristos"

FOUR

THE MIDDLE YEARS

1

THE PROPHECY OF 1922, THAT FOR MANY YEARS TO COME
life under the Rockefeller roof was destined to be neither
very quiet nor peaceful, amply fulfilled itself. With six
children either in day-school in New York or away at
boarding-school, either in college or recently out of it,
Abby Aldrich Rockefeller was living in seven widely different worlds and managing to transfer herself from one to
another with alacrity and humor.

One small boy with braces on his teeth "simply must
learn to chew in the back of his mouth"; another with soft
corns and blisters on his feet was without doubt forgetting
to wear his bedroom slippers at school since he had always
had a passion for wandering about in his bare feet. She
felt sorry that two of them at the same school were embarrassed because their collars were not like those of the other
boys and hastened to send others which would remove their
humiliation. Her daughter's first callers tarried far too
late. "I feel obliged to stay up until they go home. Poor
John thinks the hours they keep are awful and goes to bed
with many indignant feelings." On one especially confusing week-end David asked his sixty classmates for a picnic
lunch in the country, and Winthrop was "unhappily determined to have a house-party for his friends."

"I sometimes wish that I had been married at eighteen,"
she wrote her sister Lucy. "Then, having started my family earlier, I would be able to stand the wear and tear of
life a little better than I seem able to do. I have discovered

57

also that to find time to rest is one of the most tiring occupations I know."

Responsibilities and anxieties did not decrease when her sons entered college.

"I suppose colleges exist for two purposes," she wrote the least studious among them. "To train teachers and other expert people and to enrich the inner life of the average. I assume we belong to the latter group. Don't forget that we all need physical, moral, and mental discipline, and especially those of us who have much of this world's goods. You have plenty of brains if you will only use them and work whether you feel like it or not. The way to manage college as I, who never went to one, see it, is to begin to study at once before your lessons get hopelessly ahead of you."

She and their father awaited anxiously the results of examinations. They were "thrilled at breakfast" over the news that one boy had passed a difficult French examination. "We are still rejoicing," she wrote another, "over your good marks, for they show that you are really learning how to study and use your mind. I can understand how you feel, for I am always exhilarated by difficulty. My respect for the broad-mindedness of the college has been confirmed by its having put you in the First English class in spite of your spelling! I'm so happy about it that I wish I could hug you!"

Both parents agreed not only that college rules should be kept to the letter, but that good sense and discretion should govern all privileges. When one son wanted to take in one month the college allowance of two weekends in order to see Maine in October, he was refused his request. "I am sorry to disappoint you," she wrote, "but your father and I feel strongly that it would make a bad impression on the college, both on faculty and students, to have you spend two Sundays away in the first month you are there. The boys who cannot afford to go away will feel restless and envious, and your professors may well think that you are not taking your work very seriously. When you think this over, I am sure that you will agree with us."

She was deeply interested in the clubs or fraternities to which they might be elected and in their reasons for deciding upon this one or that. And with reminiscent humor she informed one of them that *she* still possessed an Alpha Delta Phi and a Psi U. pin which she would gladly lend should occasion arise. She disapproved volubly of class and fraternity hazing, thinking it dangerous and barbarous. "Of course, you will take it good-naturedly now, and in your later college years I hope you will see what you can do to moderate or abolish it." Football baffled her, although she tried valiantly to follow the games in the newspapers, secretly relieved that none of her sons was good enough at it to play on the college elevens. "I simply can't remember, try as I do, who is on which side, though I've read the line-ups over and over. Perhaps I shall do better after you have given me careful instructions."

She loved to visit them at Princeton or New Haven, Hanover or Cambridge, but she was always careful to say that she did not in the least mind their neglect of her while there, since their studies clearly took precedence. She would be quite happy by herself, just seeing the sort of life they were living and the places where they lived it.

She was often concerned over their being constantly with others. "Never having been away at school or college myself," she once wrote, "I can't imagine what it is like to be in a crowd all the time. The only way to stand it, I suppose, is to try to arrange your time so that you have some hours to do things alone. I only hope you have some quiet place to turn to. Much as I love people myself, I know it's a dangerous thing to become too dependent upon them. Everyone needs a certain amount of solitude in order to learn to know oneself and to get a grasp on things, alone."

2

HER CHILDREN'S LETTERS TO HER DURING THESE YEARS REveal a confidence in her which quite clearly allowed them complete frankness in the expression of their feelings and opinions. If they did not agree with her, they were quick to say so; if they thought her hasty in her judgments, as she sometimes was, they relied upon her honesty to accept their correction and even criticism.

Her homesick daughter at sixteen wrote from a summer camp to which, within a few days, she became completely devoted:

Oh, Mama, darling, take me away from this horrible place. Please do, for Pity's sake, or I'll die! I can't stand it. I have been wandering about hunting for a place to lie down and cry it out, but when I lay down even for a minute, I actually felt the blood running down my back from the black flies. It is perfect Hell here with these horrid, unfeeling girls. I can't ever describe to you what it is like to be without home or friends. The doctor says she thinks I look very pale. For God's sake, take me home. Whenever I think of home and then of this pepless place, I nearly blow up. If you will only let me come home, I will honestly try to live up to it. Only please tell Mrs. W— that you really *want* me at home, or *anything* except that *I* want to leave, because that would hurt her feelings.

Buckets of love,

Abby

Young Abby was equally outspoken about her new school.

You ask me how I like school. Well, I will tell you. I like the teachers and the lessons better than I did, but I do Not like some of the girls. Those of them who live in better houses and have more maids are constantly making very pointed remarks about how little the others have, and they of course don't like it and so they pretend to have things they haven't. And another thing, it seems to me that every girl in my class has a disgusting cold and no handkerchief. I am counting the hours until vacation. I can't think of anything but the trip we are going to take. Lots of love from your lonely daughter

Abby

P.S. Lonely, but soon hopes to be cheerful.

Her son John at fifteen remonstrated with her over her desire that he should go to a dance during his vacation.

I got your very discouraging letter on Monday. I can't say that I feel very enthusiastic at present about going to that dance. Mightn't we go to the country instead? It seems to be your one ambition to get me to go to dances. I suppose I *will* go if you want me to, but I don't remember the girl very well, and I do recall that she dances very poorly. Well, I will leave it up to you.

And Winthrop at fourteen wrote from his school:

Dear Ma:

The letter you wrote me by hand had a nice personal touch, but I must say the typewritten one was far more legable. If it is just the same to you, would you please dictate the others you write to me? I would get a lot more out of them. I am earning .75 a week helping in the workshop at noontime. My duties are to answer the questions that the small boys ask and show them how to square boards and the like. We had a very good sermon today. He only preached for 31 mins. That is the way it always goes. All the good preachers only talk a little while, and the poor ones would preach all day if hunger did not overthrow them.

Apparently suffering from an uneasy conscience, one boy at fifteen gave a very frank account of his business affairs, this time addressing his father.

Dear Sir:

Papa, I have been thinking pretty much about my accounts lately and have come to a plan. I think before we start I should put some facts to you and Mama. I am personally very ashamed of them. To tell the truth, I have not kept my accounts since we left Seal Harbor, which is 26 weeks. On the basis of $1.00 a week, I have had $26, 20% to give away, and 20% to save. That means I got $15.60 for spending, $5.20 to give away, $5.20 to save. My new plan, as a reminder to me, is to go without any money this term and to start out with a new book and all. As you know, $15.60 is quite a bit for me to spend.

I could, on the other hand, have made up a list of things that might have been true and might not. I know that you both would rather have me play the game fair. I will buy an account book tomorrow and show you what I can do. I am going to prove myself worthy.

In his third year at college a resentful young Rockefeller felt it necessary to defend himself against a reproof from his mother which he thought undeserved.

Dear Ma:

I realize with you the grave importance of "intellectual curiosity," "the will to do," and those other dynamic traits which you mention in your letter. I realize, too, that in my case these characteristics only too obviously need to be cultivated. However, your reference to me as your "son at college who is not doing his best," while true in the sense that I have not gotten as high marks as my brains might permit, is *not* merited, if "best" can mean an honest effort to establish a more mature sense of values. In other words, I have been trying to size up myself and things in general in such a way as to afford the maximum amount of constructive outlet to my abilities. This readjustment has interfered with my work; but I believe that I can truthfully say that this has become decreasingly true in the last weeks. I think that I am rapidly getting myself in hand and that I shall give you less cause for concern over me.

Shortly after his graduation from college another of her sons wrote her in reply to a letter in which she had expressed anxiety about his general attitude toward life.

Dear Mum:

I have read and re-read your letter. I can only assure you that you can't be any more worried about me than I am about myself. I find life just now pretty perplexing and pointless. A great many things that I do, I question. Some you know about and have mentioned in your letter, and others you don't know about, but, if you did, I know you would question them, too.

I agree with you that I lack sympathy. I think, however, that you give me too much credit when you say you don't think that I really am hard and unfeeling. I'm sorry to say that I am both of these, not naturally, but by schooling myself to be. I still feel that to take an impersonal, even cold, point of view about life is very important to sound, impartial judgment, and it certainly saves one from a lot of useless worrying.

I have no doubt that I am passing through a rather unfortunate stage. But with your advice and counsel I hope that I shall come out of it before some of these unfortunate habits become fixed. Anyway I have no excuses to make for myself.

Don't worry, Mum! We'll stick together anyway.

From your devoted, if bad, boy.

And during these formative years her five sons expressed their admiration and affection in many pleasant and exciting ways. One had a smaller form of his fraternity pin made for her in the hope that she will wear it "as a symbol of the love that comes with it." Another sent her flowers with a card inscribed, *To my best girl*, and yet another marked his bouquet, *To the belle of the party from one of her most ardent admirers*. "At present," confessed one, "I don't see any girl whom I could ever love enough to marry. I suppose I'll meet one some day. If you were only a girl, Mum, that would solve my problem! The trouble seems to be that I measure all girls by you."

When they were at home for vacations, they would rather take her out for dinner than any girl they knew. "Perhaps it is just because I'm growing up," said one of them after such a dinner by themselves, "but certainly I have never realized so keenly your incredible understanding and patience and your complete devotion to all of us. This realization, which is emotional as well as intellectual, has made my feelings toward you such that any written expression of them would sound silly. There is no one in all the world with whom I feel so free."

3

Her natural genius for discovering all manner of resources to offset family anxieties and the pressure of outside interests always came to her rescue. Detective stories upon occasion were "perfect life-savers"; sewing and knitting were "veritable godsends." She took delight in starting in her Maine garden a nursery of little seed-

lings and cuttings, vines, shrubs, and trees, which, when
the children should have homes and gardens of their own,
would be ready and waiting for them. When she was
weary of meetings, boards, and committees, she experi-
mented with cooking, giving the kitchen staff an afternoon's holiday and making pancakes for her husband
from Aunt Jemima's flour, "which turned out excellently."
She loved to arrange flowers and spent hours in teaching
the members of her household staff charming ways of
placing them in bowls and vases. She loved, too, to rear-
range a room, moving all the furniture about, rehanging
pictures, surprising everyone including herself. She adored
"escapes," an escape for a solitary walk along Fifth Avenue, studying the faces of passersby, listening to over-
heard conversations; an escape at Pocantico to watch the
geese nesting on the lake; an escape from family and
guests to the small Rest House, built as a refuge in the
Seal Harbor woods, where, after an afternoon of reading,
she and her husband could eat their supper of bread and
butter and blueberries, and wash their dishes, wrangling
pleasantly over whether, as he contended, dishes could be
washed by the hands alone, or whether, as she maintained,
a mop was necessary.

Like all the Aldriches she adored travelling, and once
the children were sufficiently grown either to be taken
along or to be safely left behind, she felt more free to be
away although she "always loved better being at home."
She never outgrew her excitement over boarding a steam-
ship, dressing for dinner "in the same dress each evening
to the secret scorn of my table-mates," receiving farewell
telegrams and flowers from her sons. "One of the nicest
things about leaving you all," she wrote during a journey
to Egypt with Dr. James Breasted, "is having time to

think of all my nice children and how fortunate I am to have you all. I feel extremely proud and happy." She was also proud and happy over playing Russian Bank on shipboard with Dr. Harvey Cushing and beating him soundly.

In 1924 she spent two "wonderful months" in France with her daughter. Secure in the knowledge that her three older sons were camping with their father in Wyoming and that her two younger were in the care of an especially reliable young tutor, she could give herself up to such pleasure as she had not enjoyed since she was a girl. Her letters to her husband during a warm and bright July in Paris were filled with excitement over entertainments arranged for her because of his generous gift toward the restoration of French historic monuments. "Everybody, high and low, loves you for it, and, of course, all these things are done for me only because I am *your wife.*" She lunched with barons, marquises, and princes, took tea with an ex-queen at Versailles, "all Royalist and all, with their strange clothes, looking as if they belonged in quite another century." She went with her daughter to the *Folies Bergères*; and on July 14th, when everyone who could afford it had left Paris for the holiday, she took some young people for a "thrilling supper of scrambled eggs and hot chocolate" at a place where the Yale band was playing and everybody was dancing. Since she was "thinner," she could dance better and enjoy it more!

Every day was "marvellous," whether she was exploring the old streets on the Left Bank of the Seine or picnicking in the Bois de Boulogne, buying some new dresses (which she devoutly hoped her husband would like) or inspecting the bathroom of Louis XV at Versailles. On July 20th she attended the "fête de Versailles, the usual celebration with a little extra for you because of your

Fanny

The Tetlows

Asenath

gift." There were the most beautiful fireworks imaginable before the fountain of Neptune with reflections in the jets of water, a display which she would never forget and which made her long for him to enjoy it with her. Young Abby and her companions, however, were not especially enthusiastic. "I simply can't understand it," she wrote. "They just don't enjoy *anything* so much as *I* do." Her French improved daily through constant use; and, since her hosts and hostesses were "such clever guessers," she made out very well with all manner of people and with every topic of conversation. She was not even dismayed by "an old, dirty, motheaten curator" at the Bibliothèque Nationale, who was "an awful liar as well" and who refused to allow her to see a certain Persian manuscript.

A three-day motor trip to the Channel coast gave her memories she would never forget although the ocean at Dinard made her homesick for Maine. The sunset at Saint Malo, Mont Saint Michel never so lovely, the cathedral at Rouen, the old French farmhouses, the long, straight roads lined with plane trees—everything was perfect in spite of one of her travelling companions who had the "worst manners" she had ever seen and "less sense." Albert, the chauffeur, on the other hand, was "clearly the nicest man in France."

In 1928 another visit to France was undertaken, this time, to her great joy, with her husband and three of her sons. The confusion which she had some reason to anticipate with two relatively young boys unused to foreign travel was pleasantly calmed at the outset. "Although we have travelled pretty hard," she wrote to her two sons remaining at home, "the boys have been splendid. Winthrop and David started to quarrel, but after one or two talks with Papa have settled into a very happy relationship. Laurance pays all the bills and settles all questions of fees with his father. He is keeping the accounts and doing it beautifully. He is now on a salary. Winthrop takes all care of the baggage, sends cables, and does other errands, also on salary. David is my *valet de chambre*, cleans my shoes, hangs up my dresses, carries my coat, etc., also on salary. This family solution is working very well for everyone concerned."

In all her letters home from whatever country she is visiting, she again and again expresses her pride and delight over her own. In Egypt, distressed and concerned over the poverty and disease of the common people, she is constantly thankful that she is an American woman. "I am every day more grateful that I belong to a land which has a future instead of a past, and a future which even *I* can help to build." And in an outburst over trends and tendencies in America which she fears, she writes:

"I love my country, and even more when I am away from it. Yes, in spite of Huey Long, Father Coughlin, and others I could name, I love her still."

4

THROUGH THESE MIDDLE YEARS, WHILE THE CHILDREN WERE growing up and while outside responsibilities and interests were also demanding her care and attention, the close association with her own brothers and sisters gave her continual pleasure. A letter to her brother Edward, written in March, 1927, and concerning a division of the furnishings in the house at Warwick Neck, expresses her gratitude and affection toward them all.

You were good enough to suggest that there might be things in the house at Warwick which I would like to have to keep in memory of Mama and Papa and which I could pass on to my children as heirlooms. Of course, there are such things. I would be glad to have any of the needlework furniture and the Egyptian head. And if no one else wants the small portraits of Grandmother and Grandfather Chapman and Aldrich, I would be glad to have them, also Mama's portrait as a young woman.

But, as I have thought over our talk on the telephone the other day, I have reached the conclusion that it is really far better that I should not be considered in connection with any division of the Warwick furnishings. This conclusion I have reached because most precious of all things to me that have come from the family is the affection and companionship of my sisters and brothers. Our feeling of family solidarity and friendship is, I am beginning to think, quite unusual. I don't believe there is one of us who would think for a minute of sacrificing the feeling of any other member of the family for any amount of furniture or money. I would not want to have anyone give up for me something he or she would like to have.

This sense of family solidarity and friendship remained throughout Abby Aldrich Rockefeller's life as one of the most valued of her possessions. Much as she loved her various brothers, Ned, Stuart, Richard, William, and Winthrop (three of whom still lived in Providence), and her sister Elsie, she was perhaps closest to her sister Lucy, unmarried and five years her senior. Frequent visits to Lucy in the old house on Benevolent Street always meant freedom and pleasure to her. Nor did she ever outgrow a love of Providence. "I am always happy to be in Providence," she often said, "where everybody calls me Abby."

From the day of Abby's marriage until the six Rockefeller children were themselves married with families of their own, Aunt Lucy never faltered in her interest and devotion. Whether she was buying clothes for her sister ("a daring pink hat," "a pale blue gown in which you will look your best, which is *very* important") or taking young Abby on a trip around the world, or presiding over the house in New York or in Seal Harbor during a necessary absence of father and mother, she was always ready for any emergency or necessity. Moreover, she provided excitement to children and servants alike. "All the staff was glad to have you here," her sister Abby wrote her after one such stay. "You see they don't usually experience such amusing and exciting things when John and I are at home." And Lucy replied after another such visit: "I have had the most wonderful time with your children, your most valuable possessions. One thing that Roosevelt can't do is to put a tax on them!"

Through all these years the library at 110 Benevolent Street was the scene of numberless conversations between the two Aldrich sisters: on the Rockefeller children and Lucy's judgments as to the assets and liabilities of each, which opinions she was neither careful to conceal nor reluctant to express; on travel, which both adored, and treasures, which each cherished; about books, upon which they often violently disagreed, and about art, upon which more violent disagreements were likely to arise. When Abby bought a certain Matisse, Lucy informed her that there must be something wrong with her character for her to have made such a purchase; when the "abstractions" in the Museum of Modern Art came up for discussion, Lucy "merely wiped them aside with a wave of her hand"; and when Picasso's value was stoutly debated between them, Lucy contended that, if a child of Abby's had remotely resembled his creations, the only possible solution to such a tragedy would be an immediate dose of chloroform! Alike in humor and vitality, they obviously enjoyed such disagreements. "Although we often argue," Abby wrote her sister, "I don't know of anyone I admire so much."

Quite aside from family ties and a relationship rare even among sisters, Lucy Aldrich was, and still is, a personality too seldom encountered on one's way through this earth, and this fact was abundantly recognized by her sister Abby. Although she had been early afflicted by deafness, Lucy had never lost a consuming interest in life and in all its manifold offerings. Her humorous acceptance of its incongruities and of its lack of accommodation to the individual, her ability to laugh at herself as well as at most others, her delight in experience for its own sake whether in Providence or Peking, her sometimes overwhelming candor, and her quick and apt turn of phrase, fill the letters which she wrote her sister and reveal her as a peerless companion. She quite clearly loved to indulge herself in ironic humor at Abby's expense, and her letters were guaranteed to provide many a laugh.

I am so sorry you have had the flu and have had such a hard time getting over it. Why don't you cut out church for a while? I don't think too much church agrees with the Aldrich family. Wasn't it Elsie who put a bone out in her spine while she was kneeling in prayer? I think it is better for us Aldriches to pray on our feet.

Nor did she hesitate to dump her discouraged moments upon her sister, sure of her understanding and her amused sympathy.

I *am* discouraged. I have had such terrible luck about everything this year. This is the first day for two weeks that I haven't had a terrible pain in my teeth. The Lord certainly made an awful mess for us when he thought up teeth! I can't hear anything, I can't see much, my two dogs have died, and I have come to the sad conclusion that all the things I bought abroad are either fakes or have disappeared. I find nothing tires me so much as trying not to get tired, but I'd rather be dead tired any time than bored to death.

Do come to Providence this week-end. If you don't, I warn you that you probably won't see me for some time. I'm likely to set out for Paris or for Heaven at a moment's notice.

Lucy Aldrich was a perennial source of excitement to the Rockefeller young. When in the spring of 1923 on a trip to China, she was seized by Chinese bandits, who boarded her train by night and kept her for a weekend in captivity, her nephews did not for a moment share their mother's alarm over terrifying cablegrams from American officials in Peking. "Don't worry about Aunt Lucy! She can look after herself." "What a kick Aunt Lucy will get out of this! I'll bet she's had the time of her life."

Their diagnosis both of their aunt and of a perilous situation which might well have resulted in disaster was apt and accurate. Lucy Aldrich at fifty-five and already quite deaf did have the time of her life as her own inimitable description of this episode bears witness.[1] Clad in a pink crepe de Chine nightgown, which the bandits greatly admired, and a thin satin wrapper, topped after some freezing hours by a purloined English jacket, she rode a mangy donkey over mountains which, she calmly observed, "resembled the Dolomites and afforded magnificent views." When the bandits poked her in the back with

[1] For a first-hand account of this adventure see "A Week-End with Chinese Bandits," by Lucy T. Aldrich. *The Atlantic Monthly*, November, 1923.

their pistols, when they pushed and pulled her over rocks and through thickets, she scolded them furiously and "bossed them about" until she had reduced them not only to decent treatment of her, but to laughter as well. She felt, indeed, vastly complimented when they communicated to her by signs that she was Number One in their estimation. Her torn and blistered feet, further lacerated by an emerald and a diamond ring which she concealed from her captors in the toes of her slippers, rain, cold, sunburn, hunger, vermin, and dirt could not daunt her spirits. When the exhausted bandits stopped for an infrequent half-hour on their wild flight, she lay down and slept beside her weary donkey since she wisely concluded that she needed all the rest possible. Upon her rescue by Chinese soldiers, she declared that she had never been frightened for a minute; and she even felt a bit sad to leave her particular bandit in the hands of the law; in fact, she patted him on the back in affectionate farewell.

5

"To be young," wrote Hazlitt, not without a spirit of bitterness in the consciousness of his lost youth, "is to be as one of the immortals." Abby Aldrich Rockefeller never felt that bitterness simply because she was apparently never conscious that she was, at least in the inconsequential matter of years, no longer young. All her life she possessed the vitality and the buoyancy of youth. "I can be broken-hearted over little things," she once wrote, "and I often am; but life with all its sadness never quite breaks my heart. I can never lose my faith in people, their possibilities, their inherent dignity." She possessed, too, other unquenchable traits of youth: its eagerness, excitement, and sense of power, its dreams and its visions, its delight in the new and the untried, even its stubborn, unyielding assurances.

Quite naturally, then, she loved young people, her spiritual contemporaries, and they in return sought after her as one who spoke their language, shared their thoughts, and understood their problems. She remained unshaken by those periods and phases which confused and confounded many of her generation: the sad young men of the post-war nineteen-twenties, the jazz age, "flappers" and "bobby-soxers." "One is constantly told that the young men and women of to-day," she said in an address given in the late twenties when three of her sons were approaching early manhood, "are less ready than their forefathers to carry on; but I believe they are every bit as ready. I like and admire the young people whom I know. Being frank myself, I am not in the least shocked by the lack of reserve in their conversation. I am delighted that girls are having a greater chance to express themselves. I love to see the old hypocrisies being shattered. I am undismayed because I believe in human nature and because I trust the power of love and of those high hopes that lie hidden in every heart."

As her sons grew older, she took delight in sharing with them her own interests, with one, her concern over the race problem, with another, her pleasure in art and her eagerness to study it. "I love being your mother," she wrote one of them on his twenty-first birthday, "and having you old enough to be a friend and a companion who shares my enthusiasms. Perhaps a mother is expected to give her sons advice on their twenty-first birthdays, but

74

I just don't feel that way. All the advice I can give you is to remember that you always have the affection and confidence of your mother. I respect you too much to want to impose my will or even my opinions upon your own. All that your father and I want is that *you* find the right path for yourself and follow it the best way you know how."

Not that she was always, or even often, able or willing to keep her opinions to herself. She was far too outspoken for such self-restraint, although her unfettered expression of what she believed never included a wish or a will to dominate. Moreover, like most persons of overflowing vitality, she held to her own principles and decisions with a sometimes irritating fervor and tenacity which not infrequently required good-humored forbearance on the part of her husband and children. Her final capitulations were, however, so good-humored in themselves and her willingness to declare herself "mistaken but still devoted" so disarming that they only endeared her to those from whom she differed. And she was ever ready to admire in others, and particularly in her children, staunch convictions and uncompromising loyalties although they were not always her own.

Her selfless devotion to her children and her honest desire that they should make their own decisions and follow the paths which to them seemed best and right were perhaps revealed at their finest when one by one they began to establish their own homes. With her own completely happy marriage behind and before her, her conviction, often expressed, that "marriage is an art and not an experiment," and her ideal of the American home as the foundation and the hope of our civilization, she was deeply and anxiously concerned over their choice of partners for this supreme adventure. "Wives and mothers need character, brains, and charm," she told her sons and devoutly trusted they would not be unaware of these requirements when they were faced with the critical hours of decision.

She wanted above all else, as she often said, to live again with the families of her daughter and her sons the life of yet another generation, knowing always that that new generation must be reared under conditions vastly different from those which had governed not only her own upbringing, but that of her children. "I'm secretly pleased, of course, when my daughters-in-law ask my advice," she wrote a friend after the last of her sons was married, "but I never give it unsolicited." Her daughters-in-law clearly found in her what many have hoped for and few discovered. "I often wish," wrote one of them, "that there were fifteen Rockefeller sons instead of just five so that there could be fourteen young Mrs. Rockefellers as blessed as I am in their new mother and father. Every day I realize how truly fortunate I am." And each new daughter-in-law never forgot the charming way in which her new mother-in-law in any family gathering apparently overlooked her cherished sons in order that her most recent daughter should feel completely at home.

Upon the arrival of her first grandchild in 1928 when she was fifty-four, she was so excited that she gave a "new grandmothers' party" for the sharing of a common pleasure. "Your father is awfully funny about being a grandfather," she wrote her sons. "He says that he doesn't like at all being married to a Grandmother, and when people call him *Grandpa*, he rather winces. As for me, I adore it!"

The assumption of parental responsibility on the part of her children afforded her secret delight, shared only with their father. "The other day Nelson gave me a long and most serious lecture upon how I should treat little Roddy. I took it, of course, very meekly, but it amused me greatly."

6

OF ALL THE SUBJECTS AND PROBLEMS WHICH AROUSED HER interest and enlisted her eager activity during these middle years, perhaps the one of most importance to her was that prejudice which she saw within the minds of many of her fellow Americans toward foreign races and peoples, creeds and colors. Nor did she see it there alone. In the years immediately preceding the First World War, when the arrival of steamships meant the arrival also of hundreds of bewildered and hopeful strangers, she had become increasingly aware of its dangerous strength in the lack of understanding of any one nationality toward the people of another. In the years which followed she became deeply concerned not only with the immediate problems of the assimilation and integration of a new population, but with the more abstract ideal of human justice, an anxious concern which was accentuated by her hopes and ideals as the mother of American children. During the nineteen-twenties this anxiety found constructive expression in her companionship and friendship with mothers of diverse origin and in various projects for their economic and social welfare.

In an address given during this period on tolerance among peoples and designed particularly to suggest ways and means by which young children might be taught freedom from racial prejudice, she spoke of the value which familiar works of art might have in such teaching. If the mind of a child could be made to understand that the pictures which gave him such pleasure were the expression of the idealism and the culture of other lands than his own, he would not be slow to realize that a love of the good and the beautiful is common to every people and that such love has through the ages bound all races and nations together. She would also train children to feel excitement and interest instead of suspicion and scorn toward a schoolmate who speaks a strange language, eats odd foods, and perhaps dresses unlike themselves. "One often feels uncomfortably," she said, "that children are peculiarly lacking in the spirit of adventure (that is, outside of pure romance) and comes to the sad conclusion that this is true because they have imbibed that spirit of criticism and doubt toward so-called 'foreigners' from parents and others by whom they are surrounded and who kill their natural idealism and destroy their confidence in all but the usual and the conventional. Since they are destined to become responsible men and women in a world where good manners, good will, and understanding must prevail, they should surely be taught in school and in church, and above all in their homes, that fair play and justice, truth and a love of humanity, are far more important for a country than mere national pride."

When her three eldest sons were in college, she wrote them a letter which gives fervent expression to her ideas on this subject and which eloquently records her hope for their own intelligent and humane behavior as American citizens.

Dear John, Nelson, and Laurance:

For a long time I have had very much on my mind and heart a certain subject. I meant to bring it up at prayers and then later have it for a question to be discussed at a family council; but the right time, because of your father's illness, has never seemed to come.

Out of my experience and observation has grown the earnest conviction that one of the greatest causes of evil in the world is race hatred or race prejudice; in other words, the feeling of dislike that a person or a nation has against another person or nation without just cause, an unreasoning aversion is another way to express it. The two peoples or races who suffer most from this treatment are the Jews and the Negroes; but some people "hate" the Italians, who in turn hate the Jugoslavs, who hate the Austrians, who hate the Czecho-Slovaks, and so it goes endlessly.

You boys are still young. No group of people has ever done you a personal injury; you have no inherited dislikes. I want to make an appeal to your sense of fair play and to beseech you to begin your lives as young men by giving the other fellow, be he Jew or Negro or of whatever race, a fair chance and a square deal.

It is to the disgrace of America that horrible lynchings and race riots frequently occur in our midst. The social ostracism of the Jew is less brutal, and yet it often causes cruel injustice and must engender in the Jews a smouldering fire of resentment.

Put yourselves in the place of an honest, poor man who happens to belong to one of the so-called "despised" races. Think of having no friendly hand held out to you, no kindly look, no pleasant, encouraging word spoken to you. What I would like you always to do is what I try humbly to do myself: that is, never to say or to do anything which would wound

79

the feelings or the self-respect of any human being, and to give special consideration to all who are in any way repressed. This is what your father does naturally from the fineness of his nature and the kindness of his heart.

I long to have our family stand firmly for what is best and highest in life. It isn't always easy, but it is worth while.

Your Mother

FIVE

THE LATER YEARS

1

From the late nineteen-twenties on, mr. john d. Rockefeller, Jr. not infrequently approached his home in the early evening with certain misgivings, fortunately tempered by amused curiosity. He never knew what strange and confusing pictures might be hanging upon the walls of his house! He frankly could not share his wife's new and absorbing interest in modern art, in those enigmatic, obscure, and distorted compositions which had begun to engage her excited attention and to claim, now and again, the places formerly held by his favorite Renaissance and Eighteenth-Century masters. Mr. Rockefeller, in short, did not care for modern art; and he remained unconverted in spite of his wife's ardent, and untiring, efforts at instruction. He did care, however, for her honest enthusiasms in whatever form they might take; and his generous willingness to provide the financial means for this particular adventure into fields mysterious and eccentric to him, was but one of many evidences of that sympathetic understanding and tolerance which marked their years together. Cubes and geometrical patterns, human figures which seemed to bear little relation to those he knew, strange objects which held, according to *her*, a meaning closed to *his* imagination, might bewilder and even depress him; nevertheless, if she saw in them some sense and purpose which he could not see, that in itself was sufficient reason not only for his forbearance but for his assistance and cooperation. And from the beginning of this novel and fervent enterprise, which was eventually to mean much both to New York and to the country at large, he lent his aid, delighted that at late middle age she could become so entranced by a fresh and untried pursuit.

Another difference of opinion, minor but arguable, was afforded by the Bible, which both loved and knew extraordinarily well. John did not like that tampering with the traditional King James Version which had resulted, he thought, in various unhappy translations into twentieth century usage and language. He liked his Bible as he had known it as a boy, the familiar phrases, the beautiful rendering of verse and chapter. Abby, on the other hand, welcomed rather than disliked those modern interpretations which often forsook the beauty of the old for the added clarity of the new. To her a greater measure of understanding on the part of readers, too few at best, compensated for the sacrifice of charm of language.

"We never lack material for lively arguments," her husband said in reference to such dissimilar tastes. "Modern Art and the King James Version can forever keep us young."

2

A RAPID SUCCESSION OF GRANDCHILDREN ALSO PROVIDED perpetual youth. "I don't quite know," she said, after ten granddaughters had added to her perennial excitement in life, "why the Lord has decided that I should have more granddaughters than grandsons, but I suppose there must be good reasons. One maybe is that it is good for me to get over my preference for little boys." "I adore being a grandmother," she wrote her youngest son after he had presented her with yet another granddaughter, "but even grandchildren in too large doses can be exhausting, and to remember the birthdays of seventeen is a major job."

Every new grandchild was heralded as though it were the first to appear, and she could not wait until she was allowed to hold it. Each to her had a distinct personality, different from all the others; and she loved to discern, in each, family features and characteristics which she insisted upon with an almost childish perversity—Aldrich eyes, a Rockefeller nose, the Aldrich temperament, the Rockefeller stability. "I love children," she wrote a friend, "and especially little ones. Always excepting my husband, my many grandchildren give me the greatest comfort and pleasure in my life. I love even their naughtiness, their funny wants and their plots to get them, which I can see lurking in their minds. Even when they are a day old, they are real people to me."

Her preference for little boys was soon satisfied by a sufficient number, and her granddaughters, two of whom were named for her, early justified their sex. "They are so simple, unaffected and natural, so healthy and robust, that they give your father and me great pleasure." She was impressed by the dexterity and skill with which the little girls used their hands. "A table came as a Christmas present for us," she wrote one of her sons, "but it was unassembled. Your father and I were terribly clumsy about how to get it together. Young Abby took hold of it and in exactly three minutes had set it up." Two of them wove some small rugs and mats for her, and she was surprised by the smoothness and excellence of their work.

Just as she had loved giving parties for her own children, she loved planning them for the third generation, soon in number enough to provide an hilarious gathering quite by themselves.

"I'm rather glad John was not present at my luncheon for his grandchildren. I'm sure he would have been shocked by our table-manners, which we sometimes forgot in the good time we were having. Also by my allowing them to sing at the table. The new waitress seemed a bit shocked herself. We had quite a grown-up conversation during lunch. I'm not sure you would call it exactly intellectual, the subject being moths, each of us telling what had happened in our houses when the moths had gotten the better of our vigilance. At any rate, I'm establishing such a reputation among my grandchildren for good food that I'm beginning to wonder what they get to eat at home."

Her desire to live again in a new generation was abundantly realized. She established early between herself and her grandchildren that ageless and easy companionship which she had given her own children. She loved nothing better than to have each grandchild for breakfast or for lunch with her alone, the two of them talking together of common interests. When they were away at camp or at school or when she was absent from New York, she found time to write them of her pride in their accomplishments, that one played basketball well, that another loved to read as *she* did, that a third had a prodigious memory for poems. She was always sending or taking them "little gifts" because she wanted them to enjoy "those little things in life which everybody can possess and cherish."

Pocantico, where her daughter and each of her married sons had a home, gave her opportunities for games and picnics with the grandchildren and for seeing them undertake new ventures. She watched them learn to ride under the careful instruction of Joe, the head of the stable, who over a period of many years taught them all and who was as loved by them as they were by him. In September, 1944, when the young Rockefeller fathers were in various theaters of war, she wrote them of the family horseshow.

Saturday was the great day of Joe's annual horseshow. I do wish you boys could have been here, for it was really a most extraordinary sight. All the grandchildren were there, with the exception of the two tiny babies, which meant that there were fifteen children milling about. All of them seemed perfectly happy and independent and paying very little attention to any of us grownups. There was a very sad lack of fathers present.

Joe had appointed your father and Blanchette [1] as judges of the show. Blanchette made all the ribbons, it must have taken her hours, and there were three awards, first prize, blue ribbon, second, red, and third, yellow. Since there were just exactly three children in each class, *everybody* got a ribbon. I have a suspicion that there was a little question in some minds as to the impartiality of the two judges; but all the children took it extremely well, and those who didn't get a blue said they would get one next year, and asked me why I wasn't a judge. I told them I was sure Joe didn't choose me because he knew that I would insist on blue ribbons for all of them!

Perhaps I was most thrilled by seeing little Lucy and David, both under four years old, riding around the ring. They were perfectly calm. David, even when he started to slip off his pony when rounding a corner, was not at all frightened, though Joe had to lift him up on his horse for a minute; and he went right back on his pony again as soon as the difficult corner had been accomplished. Another thing that impressed me was the way Marilyn rode Chico. You remember what a very nervous, high-strung horse he is, but Marilyn seemed to have a magic effect

[1] Mrs. John D. Rockefeller, III.

upon him, for he settled down and did just what she wanted
him to do. She seems to understand animals. Her mother came
only for the last half-hour because she was so afraid some of
the children would be thrown off and hurt. I have such confidence in Joe as well as in the children, and even in the horses,
that it didn't worry me at all. The show lasted three hours,
and when it ended, the children all gathered around Joe and
gave him three lusty cheers.

It really was a wonderful time, and we all missed you sadly.
I hadn't seen my four daughters-in-law together for a long
time, and I am very glad to tell their husbands how extremely
well they looked and how very proud I was of them all.

3

FOR MANY YEARS A PACIFIST, ABBY ALDRICH ROCKEFELLER
abandoned that adherence when in the nineteen-thirties
the ominous cloud of German Nazism began to darken
not only Europe but the world. In 1935 she expressed her
anxiety over the apparent lack of "any humor whatsoever" in Hitler and his henchmen and her conviction that
"a nation without humor is not only sad but dangerous."
She was outraged over reports of German concentration
camps and of the barbaric treatment accorded to the Jews.
She became troubled over the seeming apathy and blind-
ness of Americans in their attitude upon world affairs.
"I'm not only increasingly bored by hearing attacks on
the Roosevelts," she wrote in the same year, "and depressed by the bad taste that prompts them; but I am
deeply worried because people who have the brains to do
so are clearly not taking a more serious and intelligent

approach to the problems, even the dangers, that threaten not only us, but the world."

Traditionally and naturally a Republican, she was rarely bitter over political issues and often expressed admiration of the personal qualities of men with whose opinions on domestic and foreign affairs she violently disagreed. "I believe he is a sincere, honest, and upright man," she wrote of the presidential candidate of a rival party, "and even if I do not agree with his point of view, I can deeply respect him." Just as she had longed and labored for the success of the League of Nations in the years following the First World War, so she distrusted and hated the isolationist position in the years immediately preceding 1941 and was shocked by the principles and the activities of the group known as America First. Although she was critical of certain aspects of President Roosevelt's foreign policies, once America had joined forces with her European Allies she withheld any wholesale approval of his Republican rivals until she was assured of their stand upon world affairs. After the election of 1944 she hoped that a coalition cabinet of men of both major parties might be formed and that the Republicans "would forget their differences and back the country up." Her heroes in 1945 were Generals Eisenhower and Marshall. If she had been a man, she would wish to be just like Eisenhower "with all his modesty, tact, intelligence and understanding." "Except for Churchill's literary ability," she wrote, "I cannot admire him so much as I admire my two American heroes." And during the last year of her life her cherished hope and her deepest desire were for the acceptance by Congress of the Marshall Plan and for the unity and strength which, she believed, it promised to a suffering world.

Throughout the war years she was scrupulous, even adamant, in her adherence to every jot and tittle of the rationing laws. She wished men would realize how complicated and difficult housekeeping had come to be and felt a wholesale sympathy for all honest American women faced with the problem of feeding a family. Much as she liked home-made ice-cream, she served the drug-store variety for parties since her supply of sugar was exhausted, limited all dinners strictly to "three courses and no more," and had never before realized how pleasantly one *could* subsist on fish. She was "horrified, in fact nearly killed" when, at a meeting held in the Rockefeller home, someone inadvertently remarked that the number of cigarettes about (a quantity which had quite legally accumulated in a non-smoking house) suggested the Black Market. When their scanty supply of gasoline was exhausted and she "would gladly die rather than procure more dishonestly," she rejoiced in their ancient Electric at Pocantico, in the horses there, and in her feet "which have not yet failed me."

4

IN 1945 THE PIECE OF JEWELRY DEAREST TO HER WAS HER five-star pin. With four sons in uniform and the fifth appointed Assistant Secretary of State, she felt not only a justifiable pride in her contribution to her country, but also a bond with all other American mothers who could wear pins similar or identical to her own.

She had every cause to be proud of her sons. Two in the navy were advanced to the rank of Lieutenant-Commander; two, who had entered the army as privates, rose to the ranks respectively of Captain and Lieutenant Colonel, one serving in Africa, the Middle East, and Europe, the other in the Pacific. Another, appointed by President Roosevelt in 1940 as Co-ordinator of Inter-American Affairs, continued until 1945 his services with the State Department, working to strengthen the unity and joint action of the peoples and governments of the Western Hemisphere in a common defense.

From 1941 until the summer of 1945 she followed avidly the progress of campaigns on all fronts. She studied maps, grateful for any officers or stray enlisted men whom she could ask for lunch and who might enlighten her upon unknown and heretofore unimportant Pacific islands and atolls, upon the types and uses of American ships. She and her husband spent hours bending over maps together, following the course of events, "trying to guess where our most beloved are." She became enormously interested in military strategy and read everything she could find about it, begging her army sons to suggest simple books on the subject which might partially dispel her "fearful ignorance." "I spend my whole life these days," she told them, "being mystified by the army, all my time not only trying to make out insignia on sleeves, service stripes, and decorations, but in striving to understand at least something about what I suppose you call logistics." To listen to the radio was an absorbing occupation, and, since her husband disliked hearing it at strange hours, her passion for its announcements tested her powers of contrivance. She crept from her bed late at night and in the early hours of the morning "to sit on the edge of the bath-tub" in order to listen to the reports of momentous happenings. Invasions or advances in which her sons were taking part held, of course, added and fearful importance to her; and she never outgrew the childish hope that she might just possibly hear of them by name or of certain of their superior officers of whom she knew through their letters. During the invasion of Guam, in which one of her sons took part, she listened constantly for some mention of his particular division. "I still have the feeling that once in a while they might at least just *mention* the 77th."

Her powers of contrivance sometimes met with rebuffs from her sons which she was obliged to accept though not without wistful remonstrance. "Please send me the name of your commanding officer," she begged one of them upon his admission to the army as a private. "I assure you I am asking this merely out of interest and NOT because I intend to write him." "My one regret is that you do not want me to send a Christmas card to your General," she wrote another, who had been advanced to a lieutenancy and was the commanding officer of his company. "You may be right, but I am disappointed. And possibly you may be right in thinking I should not send cards to the men in your regiment whom I have not met. But anyway I want to send in your care a card for everyone just in case you change your mind and think of any who are lonely or forgotten. There may perhaps be some who will receive no remembrance at all for Christmas. And I am going to put in with the card a small comb and nail-file for *each* of your men just in case you do change your mind. I shall enjoy my vision of you sitting under some kind of tropical tree opening my boxes, exclaiming over the good things to eat, and distributing my presents among *all* your friends, from the *General* down."

Apparently young Lieutenant Rockefeller was not able to resist his mother's persuasiveness. Whether or not under a tropical tree, he did distribute her gifts, for she received a cherished letter from one of his men who "for obvious reasons" did not sign his name to it.

Dear Friend:

Thank you. These words come not only from the lips but from the heart of a soldier who thinks you are just grand. I hope you will not think me too bold in addressing you in this way, but I feel that anyone so kind and considerate as you must be a friend.

Mrs. Rockefeller, you are to be congratulated on the fine job you did in raising our commanding officer. He is a swell guy, and I speak for the whole company without one exception when I tell you we think he is tops. Never in all my life in this army have I seen a superior go so far out of his way to make things easier for his men. Until he came to our company, we were just another bunch of G. I. Joes without any pep or vigor or morale, but nowadays we all go around with a different attitude. He is just what we all needed—a shot in the arm.

I felt you would like to have a private's opinion about your son. All mothers like to hear nice things about their children. Mine does, too, but I'm sorry to say she *doesn't*, so far as *my* life in this army is concerned. All I can say is that, though like all the rest of us, I don't relish the thought of dying in this war, I hope, if I must die, your son will be my C.O. at the time.

Well, I will close, thanking you again for everything you've done to make it a Merry Christmas for us all, who are far away from home. And again, Mrs. Rockefeller, Congratulations on your fine job!

A Boy from Company H.

She liked nothing quite so much during these war years as welcoming and feeding in her home the army and navy associates of her sons, whether officers, commissioned and non-commissioned, or enlisted men. Sometimes her guests were allied soldiers, young English leftenants, Irish or Scotch sailors whose shyness vanished before her eager, friendly questions about their own homes and families. She had a particular fondness for sergeants. "I still look at every sergeant I meet with interest and sympathy. Don't forget to remember me especially to those in your regiment whom I have met. The other day in the Providence station when I went to visit your Aunt Lucy, I could not resist accosting one who, after his initial surprise and embarrassment, turned out to be a very nice and modest boy. He wore a Presidential citation and some other honors I didn't understand. I told him I especially liked Sergeants and that was why I could not help speaking to him."

Occasionally a return courtesy from some officer on leave delighted her. An invitation to the 21 Club gave her eager anticipation for days. "I am thrilled over going to the 21 Club with Major K. I think it will probably be the only time in my life that I shall ever be in a place that even approaches a night club." When the great occasion came to pass, it fulfilled all her hopes except in one particular. "The only slightly disappointing thing was that they were so considerate of your father and me that they placed us upstairs and so far away from the other diners that I couldn't see all I wanted to. Still, we had a wonderful time. I told the waiter I would like everything to eat that I couldn't have at home. 'Roast beef?' he asked. 'No,' I said. 'We raise that ourselves.' At last we decided on Vichysoisse, chicken cooked in wild rice, and a marvellous Baked Alaska with chocolate ice-cream inside it."

She never missed an opportunity when driving to pick up soldiers or sailors going her way. "We picked up a young marine officer, just what sort I couldn't make out,

and a sailor today. They looked just like two frightened
love-birds as they huddled together on the back seat. I
told them how glad we were to have them with us, but
they never said a word." Her mania for waving her hand
in trains and in stations to all sorts of men in uniform,
some for the moment not on their best behavior, brought
upon her embarrassing remarks, in which she took only
amused pleasure, "Hello there, Grandma" being perhaps
the least offensive.

In the springs and autumns of these busy, anxious years
visits to Virginia, to their small house in Williamsburg,
gave her rest and enjoyment. Nor were these divorced
from her consuming interest in the armed forces since
many troops were stationed there or in the near vicinity.
Upon noticing that these boys had no places to sit "while
they stare at the pretty girls from the College of William
and Mary," she provided benches for them; she gave
anonymously radio-phonographs to their army recreation
halls, and contributed generously to the U.S.O. A Williamsburg Thanksgiving meant a turkey dinner for twelve
enlisted men and an evening of friendliness. "If my sub-
conscious mind were analyzed," she wrote from there in
April, 1945, "you would find most of it in Africa, or the
Philippines, or Washington. Still what is left of it here
takes delight in our tulips and hyacinths and azaleas in
the garden, all now in full bloom. Your father and I walk
about and talk of you all while we look at every single
shrub and tree which we have planted. Today we have
had a most exciting time with our axes, chopping down
those old and unattractive cedars and planting some new
ones. And this morning I heard a wood thrush singing just
outside our window. I think its song is the most beautiful
in the world. I am sending you a wonderful southern cook-

book so that when you are unable to get anything very good to eat in the army, you can read all the recipes and dream of what you can eat when you are here again."

Her use of the telephone while her sons were stationed here and there amounted to reckless dissipation which she thoroughly enjoyed, but which frequently gave her husband cause for remonstrance. Just as on her sixtieth birthday in the calmer days of 1934 she had determined to give herself "an orgy of telephoning" to all her children away from home, so she now frequently indulged herself in another such orgy at an expense which tested the good sense and humor of the head of the family.

"My dear, these telephone bills are getting a bit out of hand."

"John, has it never occurred to you that you always think *your* telephoning a necessity and *mine* an extravagance?"

The telephoning continued, though occasionally even she experienced some mild qualms over the cost. "I suppose calling you up *was* a mad indulgence, but I loved it. Perhaps I'd better wait to learn the price before I do it again. I honestly didn't realize about that enormous tax the government charges me just to hear your voices. Sunday I was quite hoarse. Your father insists it was because of too much telephoning."

Her letters over four years to her sons in foreign service are almost incredible in their number and length. "Your father has an awful suspicion that you do not read them all. He gave me a bit of a lecture on Sunday on the subject of my not going to church with him. He thinks if I am able to spend all the morning writing to you, I can quite well manage church." She writes from Williamsburg, Pocantico, and New York, "where somehow I feel closest to

96

Mrs. Rockefeller in Her Wedding Gown

you with only the ocean near at hand between us," the
minutest details of family news: of tea with her grandchildren, what each said, the evidences of growth and development in each; of countless relatives and family
friends; of the forsythia in April, the coming of the birds,
the way the male swan on the lake protects his young; of
food, "a really extraordinary Southern pie without any
upper or lower crust," the present to her of a miraculous
angel-food cake, of chocolate pudding and cream puffs,
which they "would have adored." She asks them about odd
military terms, like *echelon*, which she has to look up in
the dictionary, and describes her excitement over long con-
voys on the river. She is sometimes violently outspoken
over political affairs, "the wobbliness of our State Department," the hazy minds of certain politicians, some "revolutionary ideas about the treatment of the Negroes which
perhaps I would best keep to myself," and asks them to
set her right if they disagree with her. She gives them long
accounts of her doings, a visit with their father to the
Cloisters above the Hudson where the snow "gave peace
and quiet"; a wonderful afternoon at the Metropolitan
and an equally pleasant one at the New York Historical
Society; a play given by Negroes at the Bruton Heights
school in Williamsburg where they with two friends were
the only white people in an audience of four hundred. She
writes of her delight in seeing "Oklahoma," "The Late
George Apley," and "Harvey." "Your father enjoyed
'Harvey,' too, but he asked if it proved anything. I said it
proved the importance of having pleasant people in the
world. Though the principal character was a drunkard,
he was so very delightful that you had the feeling all the
time that perhaps to be pleasant and amusing might be
more important than to be sober and disagreeable." In

97

occasional evenings at the movies Greer Garson and Greg-
ory Peck gave her a great lift. She does not feel so much
enthusiasm for Spencer Tracy. "You must not think of us
as ever bored or lonely. We find so many pleasant things
to do together, just by ourselves, that we love to stay at
home in the evenings. I knit while your father reads aloud
to me." She plans soon to take a day off to rehang her
pictures for she feels sure nothing will raise her spirits
more.

In 1944 she described in careful and excited detail her
hopes and plans for the new Veterans' Center at the Museum of Modern Art, the forming of which was her idea
and inspiration. Through expressive work with their hands
in all manner of arts and crafts she believed that average
men could be helped to forget the destruction, ugliness,
and horror they had known by designing and constructing
things beautiful and useful.

On VE Day in May, 1945, in the midst of nation-wide
rejoicing and thanksgiving she closed her own letter of
thankfulness to a son in Europe with a characteristic
sentence:

"Perhaps, after all, it is the old who have suffered most
in this war, because we have not been able to participate
in it."

5

EVEN BEFORE THE WAR WAS FULLY OVER AND HER SONS
returned to civilian life, Abby Aldrich Rockefeller entered upon a campaign of her own, which she waged re-
lentlessly until she had emerged from it battle-scarred, but

triumphant. The cause for which she fought was the painting of family portraits; and few of her endeavors more clearly reveal that tireless determination, those powers of contrivance and cajolery which always entertained and at times mildly irritated her children and their father, and before which they confessed themselves helpless.

Like all good strategists she laid her plans far in advance of their execution and began early to acquaint her victims of their certain, indeed inevitable, fate. "My mind is possessed with the idea of having portraits done of all you boys," she informed a son still in the Pacific. "You can just make up your mind that the first thing I am going to do when you get back home is to drag you over to Mr. Dickinson and have your portrait painted. You will have enough service bars and stripes to make it really exciting. Now the next thing to do is to get your brothers firmly into line."

The head of the family himself was the first to succumb. Completed in time to celebrate Independence Day in 1944, his likeness rewarded her efforts and aroused her to fresh energy. "Your father's portrait is finished. Everyone is perfectly delighted with it, even your father. He feels it is extremely good right down to, but not including his mouth. Now for the rest of you!"

The first young Rockefeller to be vanquished, easier for conquest since he was near at hand, gave her hope for the others. "This afternoon your brother David has been sitting for his portrait. It took only three hours. I hope and pray it is good because then maybe I can get Laurance to sit for his, and if I once get *him*, then I can get the rest of you."

Laurance, at last subdued, was, according to his mother, "simply delighted with his portrait, perhaps because he

99

says it is very much better-looking than he is. His wife thinks, however, that there is too much of a hump in his nose. That can, of course, be rectified. With their good example I am sure you others will not refuse me."

Since capitulation was clearly the order of the day, the others fell into line with the exception of one recalcitrant, who steadfastly refused obedience until his mother should herself undergo the ordeal which she had forced upon them all. There clearly being no way out, she began a succession of sittings, the trials of which occasionally dampened her spirits.

"I confess I am somewhat depressed about my portrait. There is something queer about the mouth as Mr. D. now has it. It makes me look as though I smelled something slightly unpleasant. Since the woman in the apartment opposite us, in the direction I have to face in order to get the best light, dresses and undresses in front of her window and is not at all good-looking, I am not surprised. Also Mr. D. is at present a bit flustered because bluejays are attacking his vegetable garden just when he is about to add a body to my head."

The frank comments of her family did not always lend encouragement, nor did her husband's plans for providing assistance to the artist inspire her with confidence.

"Your father thinks the expression in my eyes is not right. He seems to feel that he will be able to bring into them the expression which he likes if he comes and talks with me while Mr. Dickinson paints. Personally I have grave doubts about this, and I am sure it will drive poor Mr. D. perfectly frantic."

At long last, however, the warfare was accomplished, the aggressor having perhaps paid more dearly than any of the conquered. The artist was abundantly justified in

his labors; the bluejays ceased their troubling; even the
critical Aunt Lucy was enthusiastic; and the portraits
hanging upon her walls furnished yet another proof to
their instigator that once one's mind was indomitably set
upon anything whatsoever, it could usually be brought to
fulfillment.

6

SEAL HARBOR DURING THE EARLY YEARS OF THE WAR HAD
seemed too remote from war interests and service, too far
away for boys on sudden and unexpected leaves. But in
the summers of 1944 and those following she returned
there, to the view of islands, mountains, and rocky head-
lands which she loved. "I think I am never really happy
unless I am near water," she wrote in that incomparably
clear August of 1944. "And I am convinced that there is
no air in the world like the air of Maine. The ducks are
again on Long Pond, the horses kick up their heels in
Joe's meadow; the sunrises and the sunsets over sea and
hills seem lovelier than they have ever been. Every day
is a gift, and I hate to see each go." Perhaps she knew in
some strange way that the loan of days granted to her was
running out and that the time of payment was not far off.

She had never loved her garden more as she tried to get
it back to its former state of perfection, "although Nature
this summer is clearly not working with me." She spent
hours by her lily pool, looking upon her labors, reading
with her husband under the trees. It was a quiet summer
with few people about; and they had long days by themselves, picnics in the woods, drives behind the horses along

the mountain roads with the sea below them. She was interested in the village boys and girls who had grown up during her three years of absence. "I must say I have fresh hope for our country when I see what nice, bright young people even a small village like this can produce. They are a fine lot, and I like to hear their plans for the future. One girl told me today that her brother 'of course will be a carpenter.' I said I couldn't think of anything better to do than to help build good houses for good American families to live in."

On V-J Day in August, 1945, she and her husband were spending the afternoon in the Rest House when they heard the bells ringing from the Mount Desert Island churches. "After one quick hug we stood transfixed in the middle of the room and listened to the radio, for which even your father at that moment was thankful. Perhaps there will never be again an hour like that one."

Nor was there ever a better supper than the blueberries and bread and butter which they shared at six o'clock.

SIX

EXPERIMENTS IN AMERICAN LIVING

ABBY ALDRICH ROCKEFELLER KNEW HER BIBLE. AMONG all its manifold characters whom she revered, she felt a kinship with those prophets of ancient Israel, who, distressed by the necessities and injustices of their times, strove to awaken in their people a knowledge of the demands made by God of one man toward another, simply because all share a common life, all are beset by the same sorrowful questions of human existence. The verse in the Bible, which to her summed up these demands and in its few words defined religion as she conceived it, was that spoken by the prophet Micah to his indifferent countrymen: *And what doth the Lord require of thee but to do justly, and to love mercy, and to walk humbly with thy God?* These words she often quoted to her children; and, once the six of them had reached ages which gave her more freedom, she sought to fulfill in larger measure those requirements, which, she believed, were timeless, unyielding in their application to all, and not to be carelessly set aside.

Throughout the nineteen-twenties and thirties she set forth upon certain adventures and experiments in American living, pursuing each with that boundless vitality which always seemed incredible to those who knew her and with unquenchable confidence in the powers, latent or realized, in all normal human beings to achieve the best within themselves. These dreams and visions, never divorced from practical ways and means, filled her middle years; and to each she gave unstinted devotion and that

105

gay and buoyant sense of life which threw a peculiar radiance over all her works and days.

1

WHEN YOUNG MR. ROCKEFELLER IN 1901 WAS TAKEN BY surprise over his fiancée's quick disposal of his wedding gift to her, he could at least feel some measure of satisfaction in its recipient. For she gave it to the Young Women's Christian Association of Providence, an institution in which she had shown an early and eager interest. Nor did this interest slacken after her marriage, but instead found expression in those wider fields of service represented by the National Board of the Y.W.C.A. in New York, with which she was intimately connected for many years.

Her love of people and her faith in them, their potentialities and their inherent worth as individuals, quite naturally drew her toward an organization dedicated to their welfare. Its world-wide outlook, which embraced all races and nationalities and the representatives of all faiths, appealed to her own religious views, uncurtailed or bounded by the creeds or the tenets of any one persuasion; and its labors for the social, economic, and political rights of women enlisted her support and service. Perhaps its uncompromising stand on civil liberties for minority groups, their personal safety and security, their right to vote without pressure or intimidation and to receive equal treatment in public places, and, above all else, its work for full equality of opportunity in education and in employment were the strongest influences which brought forth her time and her effort for over twenty years.

From the First World War, when the Association became deeply concerned over the activities of women in munition factories and in army camps and later in their contribution to the relief and rehabilitation of devastated areas, until the years immediately preceding the Second World War, she was a member of its National Board, serving as its vice-president and as chairman of many of its committees, including its World Service Council. She was always particularly interested in its Inter-racial Council and welcomed to her home numberless people of many nationalities in order to talk with them of their problems either in their own countries or in the land of their adoption. Her genius for understanding human beings and for instilling confidence in them, her strong and definite convictions of what was right and what was wrong in human relations, her complete freedom from prejudice, and her never-failing humor made her an invaluable member of any group which sought the improvement of undesirable or unfair conditions for women in industry and which strove for larger educational opportunities both at home and abroad.

From the beginning of her connection with the Association she refused to lend her name alone to its work, to hold merely nominally an office or membership on any committee. If she could not find time for active service, she would not masquerade under an official title. From 1918 to 1936 she did find the time and gave not only hours in conference and council, but also those executive and administrative gifts which made her leadership outstanding. And even after her necessary retirement from office on the National Board in 1936, she continued as one of its honorary members to lend her support and her encouragement.

"She was a statesman," one of her associates said of her, "with a creative vision which saw far ahead to the ultimate goal and yet with a diplomacy which never failed to take into account the immediate practical ways and means to any desired end. She had an extraordinary ability not only to grasp and to hold a mass of intricate details, but to set them in order, discarding ruthlessly the impertinent, rearranging the necessary so that they might be sharply seen and studied. Her personality was of even greater value than her executive gifts and never ceased to astonish us. She could saturate a situation immediately not only with a vitality which most of us lacked, but with a kind of stubborn hope and faith which simply would not be downed by any manner of difficulty. She literally believed that no obstacle was insurmountable; and when she entered a room either to conduct a meeting or to take part in a discussion, we all came to new life. By a sudden turn of phrase or some apt and often ironic comment she could make a roomful of discouraged women burst into laughter. She could be at any moment both earnest and funny, serious and gay; she was forceful and outright, yet in an odd and appealing way peculiarly shy about her own powers and often reticent about expressing her opinions. She could make the insecure among us fearless, infuse the faithless with conviction, and even transform a plain person into an attractive one. And not the least of her gifts was a face that might have launched a thousand ships, topped by a hat which sent us all home convinced beyond a doubt that beauty, gaiety, and daring were in themselves incalculable assets to the Young Women's Christian Association."

No job to be done was ever beneath or above her attention or performance. With equal grace she could send towels, soap, and fly-swatters to a Japanese school or discover anxious girls or women who were in need of financial help or human encouragement. She could write to the Secretary of Labor concerning minimum wages, inform the United States Government through its Secretary of War that better housing was imperative for young actresses sent to military camps to provide entertainment for soldiers, even assure the entertainers themselves that the Y.W.C.A. had far more concern over how they lived and what they ate and where they could receive their young men than it had to "pray over them," a terror which, from the very name of the Association, not infrequently assailed newcomers. When she was worried over some objective which she had set her heart upon, she could write such a disarming letter to a powerful governmental executive that he became mellowed and acquiescent even before he saw her.

"I have been ill since before Christmas, which means I am having a beautiful time playing with the children and my husband. It also means that I have had a lot of time to think. My mind has frequently wandered to the subject of our friend, the President of the United States, perhaps I should rather say *your* friend, and his attitude toward certain of our common problems. I am dying to impart these thoughts to you, but, being discreet, I do not feel like putting them on paper. If you will only come to luncheon with me some day, I will unburden my mind on these important matters with much pleasure to myself. Since this unburdening will probably have *no effect at all* upon you, you may feel sure the occasion will be quite harmless."

For many years, from 1918 on, she was Chairman of the Housing Committee of the War Work Council of the

Y.W.C.A., a committee which was organized in the critical years of World War I to help provide, through cooperation with Governmental Agencies, better living conditions for women engaged in various forms of industry. This matter of housing was of peculiar interest to her since a house and what went on within its walls was always an idea and an ideal even more than it was an exciting actuality. Nevertheless the outward and visible signs of those inward and spiritual graces which, to her, alone constituted a home held their excitements also; and she could fall as much in love with blueprints as with any other work of art. In fact, her extraordinary ability to read them and to criticise their shortcomings confounded the architect engaged to erect the house built in 1918 in Charleston, South Carolina, by the Y.W.C.A. as a home for girls working in the naval uniform factory there. She had definite and extremely practical ideas on the minutest details of such a building, on the efficient utilization of every inch of space, on the planning of kitchen sinks and the effective pitch of drainboards above them, on broom-closets and toilets, gasplates, and cross draughts to eliminate smells; and in her carefully formulated and enthusiastic plans to the Secretary of War, which she wisely sent to him in ample time for his scrutiny before her appearance in his Washington quarters, she could make a set-tub and an electric iron for girls short on clothes seem as important as a military engagement. Recognizing shrewdly the powers of personal persuasion, she eagerly undertook several such journeys to the Capitol, taking pleasure in the thought that when matters got discouraging and hope dimmed for a brief season, "there was always an ice-cream soda just around the corner."

In October, 1921, there opened in Washington a hotel

for women, known as the Grace Dodge Hotel. It was built and operated by the Y.W.C.A. and named for the first President of its National Board. Its construction had been started some years earlier, but because of building difficulties was not completed until three years after the Armistice. Originally planned to ensure decent and pleasant living quarters for women war workers in an overcrowded city, it continued to function as a home for business and professional women and for transients in Washington. Later, as its reputation grew, it opened its doors to men also. From 1921 until 1937, Abby Rockefeller was not so much its patron as she was the prime mover of its destiny. She chose its director, with whom she worked in close cooperation, studied its financial reports, and scrutinized its advertisements with a keen eye for their honesty and good taste.

She became, indeed, so consumed with plans and ideas for this hotel that Grace Dodge became a household word, and not infrequently a wearisome one, in the ears of the Rockefeller family. These ideas sprang first from her knowledge of women, their needs and desires, their financial status in comparison with that of men, their temperaments, even "those undesirable traits in them which make the average landlady prefer men as tenants of their rooms and boarding houses." She knew that, married or unmarried, women crave the atmosphere of a home, are more sensitive than men to untidiness, confusion, bad taste in furnishings; and long before the walls of the hotel were erected, she was making detailed plans to ensure that atmosphere.

Nothing escaped her. A beauty parlor was as essential as a garden where trees could be enjoyed and tea served. Pongee curtains for the restaurant were quiet and durable and could be dyed when the household tired of them. Vases and lamps "which give the impression of having suddenly escaped from a gift shop" simply would not do. The designs on slip covers might easily cause either pleasure or depression and must be carefully studied and chosen. Tired women who arrived with babies were to find rooms equipped for mothers, with cribs installed, heating appliances for formulas, a supply of diapers and nursing bottles, and helpers on hand to look after small children when either shopping or sight-seeing was desired or when a mother needed a few hours to herself with a book. Rates were to be kept moderate, and no tipping was to be allowed, an innovation which in itself created a sensation throughout the country. Smoking was to be permitted in spite of vigorous protests from several Temperance organizations and the more conservative of churches.

She knew many of the employees on the staff, who, always well-treated, continued with the hotel for years; and she delighted them upon her visits by never forgetting their names, Sam, the doorman, Irene, the chambermaid allotted to her. She insisted on clean and attractive rooms for all of them, upon fair hours for work, the best possible wages. She organized a system by which labor was divided into definite departments, supervised by heads who made their own monthly reports to the management and to her. She knew the value of money and early determined that the hotel, though a home, was not, therefore, a philanthropy. It could be run on a business basis, and it was. She objected as violently to a reference to the colored staff as "darkies" as to any discrimination in wages, status, and living quarters between them and other employees. Each Christmas she provided a party at which a concert of Negro spirituals was proudly given by the colored staff before a large audience of residents and outside guests and after which the performers were as proudly served supper by staff members who chanced to be of another color.

She knew the hotel from roof to cellar and loved to make a tour of ruthless inspection of kitchens, furnace rooms, and laundry. She could not tolerate untidiness or confusion in any of its departments, and, if a single employee was dissatisfied or disgruntled, she discovered the reason and sought to make things right. When the able woman who for years managed the hotel once remonstrated with her on the expenditure of too much care and concern "over trifles," she was unconvinced.

"I've learned that the discontent of even one person in a common job isn't a trifle," she said. "It may start as one, but it has a way of becoming an atmosphere. I've always been afraid of atmospheres myself."

Two of the Rockefeller sons have reason still to remember the Grace Dodge Hotel. Once on a visit there, when they were respectively eleven and fourteen, their mother proposed that they operate the mangle in the basement laundry during a shortage of help. They say they did a pretty good job during two hot Washington days. They each got an ice-cream soda in payment.

2

IN THE EARLY YEARS OF HER MARRIED LIFE SHE CONCEIVED the idea that, even in New York, it was not impossible to be keenly aware of one's neighbors, their natures and the circumstances under which they lived. The neighborhood with which she concerned herself was a considerable one in size, extending east from Fifth Avenue to the river and bounded roughly north and south by 54th and 86th Streets. The neighbors included various sorts of new Americans, Italians, Irish, Hungarians, Czechs, and those of other races, both Protestants and Catholics, all representing every manner of employment and many frankly bewildered by a new life in a strange country, a life vastly different from those which they had known.

Through the Fifth Avenue Baptist Church and its successor at Park Avenue and East 64th Street, both of which the Rockefeller family attended before the beautiful tower of the Riverside Church rose above the Hudson to receive their congregations, she found her opportunity for getting the neighbors together. By her initiative and leadership and with the cooperation of the women of the Bible Class of which she was the inspiration for many years, a Good Fellowship Council was formed to which all persons of any nationality in the neighborhood were warmly welcomed. Beginning as an organization for women, it soon included men as well. By the early nineteen-twenties this Council had drawn within itself several smaller community groups already formed in the vicinity by Italians, Hungarians, Czechs, and Irish, the Lenox Hill Hungarian Club, the Neighborhood Civic Club of the Czechs, the Italian Welfare Club, the United Community House on East 63rd Street.

From the beginning she was Chairman of the Good Fellowship Council, presided over its monthly meetings, and was a frequent visitor at entertainments and dinners of its diverse community clubs. The monthly meetings of the Council, which took place at the Park Avenue Church and were attended always by three or four hundred people, held open discussions on neighborhood problems with the purpose of improving living conditions. When the first of its objectives, the securing of adequate traffic lights on First Avenue, had been accomplished, it proceeded to problems of district sanitation, housing, schools, the soft coal menace, the physical safety and welfare of children at play, and other matters of common interest and necessity. Nor were the meetings always given to discussion only. Speakers were often introduced, the President of the American Federation of Labor, doctors who spoke on the better health of babies and young children, authorities who explained the immigration laws, architects who gave practical suggestions on the improvement of shops and tenements. Others came who were concerned with the culture of the human mind, with that "good life" of the intellect and of the spirit, Dr. Lorado Taft of Chicago, Dr. George Vincent, President Mary Woolley of Mt. Holyoke College. Some evenings were enriched by music, a concert by the Italian Choral Group or by Hungarian musical clubs; others, by plays acted in foreign costumes and spoken in foreign tongues.

Self-centered and strongly nationalistic as certain groups of her neighbors were, her warmth and personality by degrees banished their early suspicions, overcame their natural clannishness. She was immensely elated when the Lenox Hill Civic Club and the Lenox Hill Welfare Club combined to give, for her and her husband, a Bohemian dinner consisting of roast pork, dumplings, and sauerkraut with such a quantity of apple strudel for dessert that only a Virginia Reel could restore the physical well-being of hosts and guests alike. The Italian Welfare Club, not to be outdone, featured a dinner of spaghetti in her honor and took hilarious delight in teaching her the most adroit ways of winding it about her fork. At the Hungarian dinner on Lenox Hill she enjoyed the unfamiliar foods, and at the close of the party whirled about in the Czardas to the spirited music of Brahms' Hungarian Dance. In their turn she and her husband were hostess and host while the fascinated young Rockefellers served the refreshments and later watched their father and mother perform all manner of odd dances under the amused instruction and example of their guests.

3

INTERNATIONAL HOUSE, BUILT AND FURNISHED BY FUNDS contributed by her husband, afforded yet another outlet for her perennial friendliness toward newcomers to the country, for her anxious concern that they might be made welcome. She felt an absorbing interest, mingled with a frank curiosity, in the countless foreign students who continued to find in that beautiful and gracious building high above the river not only an attractive American home, but also the best of opportunities to mingle with those of every other nationality and thus to become at least partially familiar with civilizations different from their own.

In a letter to President Eliot of Harvard, written in 1924 when International House was opened, she expressed her hope for such friendly association among young people of every land. "John and I are deeply interested in the problem of making better international relations, and we are very happy to have the opportunity of serving this cause. We feel that this house will really strike at the root of the matter by improving interracial knowledge and

116

sympathy. Surely if the future leaders of all countries are brought together in this way while they are still young, there must be a new understanding which will contribute to the peace of the world."

Once the building was erected, she became chairman of its Furnishing Committee. She was determined that the first impression felt by a stranger from any strange land who opened its doors must be not merely one of contentment and peace, but "of a quality both human and spiritual in its pervading atmosphere." Since the house was to be the American home of its foreign guests and to most their first experience with American life, she wisely decided that the beginnings of that life in terms of its colonial past should form the theme and the motif of its interior. For its Assembly Hall she adapted the overhanging galleries of the old Beneficent Street Church, which she had attended as a girl in Providence; for its Home Room she used the wide floor-boards, recessed windows, panelled walls, and corniced ceilings of the best early American homes; even in its bedrooms she selected with utmost care and taste both the furniture and the colors and fabrics used as background and accessories.

For nearly twenty-five years she was herself the influence and the atmosphere in the many rooms, large and small, of International House, and, consciously or unconsciously, within the new lives and experiences of the thousands of diverse young people gathered together there. Her own home was theirs also. Each Christmas she and her husband gave a party for a hundred of them of many backgrounds, of every creed and color, most of whom had but recently arrived in America. Her living-rooms on that evening presented a cross section of the world at large, a confusion of tongues perhaps like that in the upper room at

117

Jerusalem, but with the same spirit that pervaded there.

A few days after her death a student from Iran, who had come to this country in 1929 and remained here, wrote to her husband of such a Christmas gathering at the house on West 54th Street.

"I first met your wife on Christmas Day nineteen years ago. I had been in this country for only a few weeks, and I was homesick, lonely, and depressed. I think she realized my loneliness, for she at once devoted herself to me, giving me far more than my share of her time, and in less than an hour I was a different boy. I shall never forget that day so long as I live, or her face, radiant with kindness and affection. She said she was an admirer of the art of my country, asked me questions about it, and pleased me greatly by commenting on my knowledge of it. We talked particularly, I remember, about Persian miniature paintings, of which she had made a study.

"One of our twelfth century Persian poets has written

O sa'di! a man of good deeds never dies.

There are few people, I believe, to whom this line can truly apply. She was one of them."

4

IT WAS, HOWEVER, ON THE GRAY, SMOKE-COVERED FLATS of New Jersey, in the midst of industrial plants and oil refineries, that Abby Aldrich Rockefeller established and achieved her most intimate experiment in American living, that which was at once most far-reaching in its influence and at the same time nearest to her heart. It was here that she put most completely into practice her faith in the American home as the stability of our country, and especially her hope and confidence in those new roof-trees being framed in a land strange to their builders, in those new roots daily being sunk in unfamiliar, untried soil.

In Bayway, a part of the city of Elizabeth, on a small plot of ground one mile long and a half-mile in width, the Standard Oil Company (New Jersey) had built some fifty small houses for the rental or the ownership of its employees. Here, upon an oasis of green grass and trees, which she would make possible, even though it was surrounded on all sides by the ugliness and confusion of modern industry, she determined in 1919, with the permission and approval of the Company, to design and construct a model workman's cottage. A letter to her sister Lucy in that year outlines her plans for such a building and suggests her hopes for what it might mean to the Polish, Lithuanian, Russian, and Czech families of Bayway, whose breadwinners worked in the plants and refineries there.

"You probably know that during the last two or three years I have been much interested in building a model workman's house at Bayway. I have gotten an architect to help me with the plans, and we have worked out what seems to me a really excellent design for a five-room cottage. One day week before last I went out there and selected possible spots on which to build this. The officials of the Company have been extremely nice and seem really glad to have me do this. I shall put my cottage alongside those that they have built, which will be a good test for it. In addition to its five rooms, it will have a bath and a small sewing-room. I plan to secure a domestic science teacher, a trained nurse, and, perhaps, a social worker, who will use my cottage as a center of demonstration to show how an attractive American workman's home can be economically and practically managed."

She laid the cornerstone of her cottage in October, 1920. It was opened the following year and known from the start as the Bayway Community Cottage. For she became at once aware that there was a greater desire and need in Bayway for a house for community activities than for the model of a possible home. To her cottage flocked so many people that its original aesthetic purpose was forgotten in the practical activities to which the immediate necessities of human beings at once dedicated it. Bayway girls began to clamor for cooking-classes in its small kitchen; Bayway women wanted a Mothers' Club in its living-room where they might bring each week for counsel and advice their confusing problems in this new country; Bayway babies voiced, if quite unconsciously, the crying need of a clinic for them in its upstairs bedrooms.

The baby clinic from the first delighted its surprised founder, who could never resist a baby whatever its origin. To its cramped quarters she went often to hold newly arrived American babies with wide Slavic faces and unpronounceable names, Zduleczna, Zydzik, Zendarska, while anxious, astonished mothers watched a doctor, provided by the city of Elizabeth, perform all manner of strange rites upon their infants and pass opinion upon their fitness as future American citizens.

"I held twenty-five naked, squirming babies today in our new baby clinic at Bayway," she wrote her daughter in 1921, "some of whom took the occasion to drench me thoroughly. Most of them were fat, rosy, and cheerful, but once in a while they all began to howl at once. I had a wonderful time. Certainly Bayway is a very healthy and progressive neighborhood so far as its babies are concerned. I thoroughly enjoyed meeting all the mothers who, though they spoke very little English, were like all mothers everywhere."

She herself chose the able and imaginative women who for years have managed the Community Center, acted as counsellors and friends of the people of Bayway. She chose, too, the bright and daring colors of walls, curtains, and chair-covers, which made her cottage the lodestone for those who had known and loved bright colors in their homelands. First and foremost a mother herself, she came to the Mothers' Club meetings in the gay living-room where there was always plenty of sandwiches, cakes, and coffee. "There's nothing like food eaten together to make people talk," she said. She confided to the Bayway mothers her problems, her mistakes and triumphs with her own children, gave advice, counsel, and sympathy. Knowing that the common possession of children was the best means of breaking down racial and national barriers and suspicions, she watched from year to year women from diverse backgrounds become American mothers, bound by the common bond of their youngsters, who raced noisily through the rooms of the Center, played and quarreled on its playground, and yet shouted at one another in one language, however new and strange.

In 1926, when her model cottage was bursting at its seams, she and the Standard Oil Company together built a Community House adjoining it. The larger house held a club-room, an ample kitchen, a better-equipped baby clinic, and a gymnasium. The cottage now was used as an office for social workers and for all overflow groups

who found no other place to go. This new Community
House welcomed to its rooms and its activities all residents
in the vicinity whether or not employees of the Standard
Oil Company. It was thus a community center in truth.
In 1939, since seams were still bursting because of the
five hundred men, women, and children who thronged
the Community House and cottage every day and evening,
yet another addition was provided, which boasted eight
bowling alleys for the men of Bayway and nearby dis-
tricts, new club and game rooms, a larger and more modern kitchen. Outside, land was found for basketball and
for more extensive playgrounds for children. In 1947, the
Company, now convinced beyond a doubt of what the
enlarged Center meant both to its own employees and to
others, decided to maintain the buildings in Bayway at
its own expense. In that year ninety-seven thousand people had made grateful use of them in one way or another.

Perhaps a quick remark, made in the early years of
Bayway Community Center by its founder to an important
official of the Company, who was dining with her, had
remained uncomfortably in his mind.

"I went to see your new cottage today," he had said at
the close of dinner over his coffee.

"Don't you mean *your* cottage?" she asked.

Abby Aldrich Rockefeller loved her frequent visits to
Bayway. She knew most of its women by name and their
children. During the dark years of the depression, when
discouragement and possible disaster were harrowing
many families, she brought encouragement and hope.
"She used to tell us in those hard years," said a Bohemian

The Children

woman, "that even though bread was important, we did not live by bread alone, and we all understood what she meant." In those years she brought pictures from her own collection to the cottage and the Community House so that her friends there might enjoy them, leaving them there for a month, then exchanging them for others. When she heard of exceptionally bright boys and girls who could profit by further educational opportunities, she made these available. And from the beginning of her absorption in the Bayway Center (for there was always within her a vein of practical, even of adamant, determination) she had the sense and the vision to allow, indeed to expect, those who made use of it to contribute weekly as they could toward its upkeep and success, realizing that in no other way could it be truly a nucleus of community life.

The Bayway young men in World War II proudly displayed on ships and in army barracks friendly notes and gifts from her. She did not forget one of them. Young people who were about to be married chose the furnishings of their new homes with her advice in mind, remembering how she had said that even one tasteful and beautiful object in a house, a good picture, a piece of lovely china, a chair or a table of beautiful workmanship, redeemed it from being merely four walls and a roof. Slavic housewives upon her suggestion taught their American daughters not to forget the old country foods and were proud when she not only ate their odd breads and cakes with relish, but congratulated them and their children upon this preservation of the old ways in the midst of the new.

Perhaps, indeed, her greatest gift to Bayway, a gift still recognized by its citizens, was her understanding of the heartaches, bewilderments, and anxieties of transplanted people, reared in old lands, suddenly transferred to a new. By that quick intuition characteristic of her, she understood their insecurity and shyness, their early homesickness, the constant tug upon them of the ties of home, of those old loyalties and customs of civilizations longer and, in some ways, richer than our own. She knew, too, the values of these loyalties as contributions to the variety and the wealth of our own culture; and, although she wanted for their inheritors the best which America had to offer in terms of improved economic status and social welfare, she longed also to preserve those gifts and graces, those memories and affections which lay deep within the imaginations of the foreign born and reared.

More important, then, to her than her model cottage and its added buildings, than the teaching within them of new household management, of better food and more tasteful dress, of the more intelligent care of children, was the discovery of the minds of the women and men of Bayway, the thoughts and dreams, ambitions and hopes which they nurtured and cherished. Nor was this discovery difficult since she could draw from them the same confidence which her East Side neighbors and the students at International House were in the same years granting to her.

"It was never what she did for us, though that was very much," a Bayway woman, who had been born in Poland, said a year after her death. "It was not even what she taught us, though she taught us many new and good things. There was something inside her that got quick inside us and made us cry and laugh at once. What was inside her somehow knew the things that were inside us.

That big thing inside her knew when we were homesick and afraid and when we worried because our children got American too soon for us to catch up with them. That was what it was even if I don't know well how to say it right."

SEVEN

ART IN OUR TIME

Unless one is careful to recall those fundamental, immovable convictions which shaped the thinking and the actions of Abby Aldrich Rockefeller, one may at first discern a seeming discrepancy between her eager participation in various experiments in American living and that consuming interest in modern art, which, during the same crowded period of her life, drew from her such ardent enthusiasm, such tireless energy. Between the manifold projects of the Young Women's Christian Association, the material and spiritual needs of newcomers to the country, whether at International House, along the East River, or on the New Jersey flats, and that radical, revolutionary movement in artistic expression, which to many suggested madness and to more bewilderment and confusion, there might seem an impassable gulf. There was, in point of fact, no gulf at all. These interests had an identical origin within her. All were equally related to her faith in the civilization and the culture of her day and of the future; all alike sprang from her own way of looking at life, which, in itself and according to its nature, must forever mean the triumph or the failure of every individual.

Her love and knowledge of art had their beginnings while she was yet a girl in her father's devotion to it; and both were increased by her familiarity with the treasures of European as well as of American galleries. This early attachment was aesthetic, perhaps even romantic, in character, an attachment far removed from that longer,

129

broader view which actuated her in later years. Art only for art's sake was neither the emotion nor the entire explanation of her zealous ardor for the distinctly new and startling in modern forms of expression. There was as well a principle, an idea, which impelled her labors for a Museum of Modern Art in New York and which at once supplemented and complemented her deep-rooted and profound conviction concerning the value of art as art. "To me art is one of the great resources of my life," she wrote in the year before the Museum was founded. "I believe that it not only enriches the spiritual life, but that it makes one more sane and sympathetic, more observant and understanding, regardless of whatever age it springs from, whatever subjects it represents."

Her own sanity and sympathy, her quick understanding of the human mind, its wants and its powers, lay behind and within her early efforts and struggles for the Museum. She believed devoutly in her own time, in the creative gifts of its people, especially of its young, and in the certain and revealing patterns of modern life which lay buried beneath its apparent confusion. She held tenaciously to a passionate faith in the new and the untried which no extreme phases of the modern movement in art could daunt. She longed to break down the misconceptions and prejudices of conservatism and convention and to extend the frontiers of human imagination. "My mother," her husband once said, "was given to a typical question: *We have always done this. Why should we do anything else?* But my wife's typical question was: *We have always done this. Why not do it in another way, or, better still, why not do something else?*"

A zest for discovery was constantly urging her on. She wanted to discover and to give recognition to young artists who were doing fresh and original work, regardless of whether such work might lie beyond the limits of her own personal appreciation or even of her approval. She wanted even more to have the ordinary man discover that art in any of its forms is neither alien to his interests nor beyond his comprehension and enjoyment. It was, then, the enrichment of human life through art which was the prime incentive for her struggles and labors to attain the new Museum, the banishment of dullness and indifference from one's allotted threescore years and ten; it was, in fact, the same desire and vision which had resulted in those other endeavors for human advancement and satisfaction.

Nor was she for a moment unaware that such pioneering, even in an age of experiment, would meet with cynicism and resistance. She knew that in the minds of many, perhaps of most, the customary, the traditional, was safe whereas the new, the untried, inevitably brought forth suspicion, criticism, and fear. Perhaps, indeed, that love of combat which she always felt when she was once convinced that the cause for which she fought was right and just was not the least of the motives impelling her early in 1929 when she put on her armor against the forces of indifference and reaction.

"Mother loved a good fight," a son said of her when, a few days after her death, the officials of the new Museum met to show her gratitude and honor. She did love a good fight; and, as in all the other lists which she had entered, she never for an instant harbored the slightest doubt of ultimate victory.

1

SHE WAS NOT, AS HAS SOMETIMES BEEN STATED, THE ONE founder of the Museum of Modern Art. That distinction was shared with others. Yet she was unquestionably the spark which set its machinery in motion, and her imagination and her endeavor were largely responsible for its final realization.

In May, 1929, she gave a small, but fateful, luncheon party in her home. Her guests were two New York women, Miss Lillie Bliss and Mrs. Cornelius Sullivan, and Mr. A. Conger Goodyear, the president of the Albright Gallery of Buffalo and a modern art enthusiast. Mr. Goodyear had met neither his hostess nor his fellow guests and had no slightest inkling as to why he had been invited to lunch. They, however, knew quite well the reason for his presence, had, in fact, laid far in advance their plans for this signal and momentous occasion.

Miss Bliss, who for many years had been eager for the founding of such a museum, had long been an apostle of modern art and an early collector of it. Her devotion as well as her collection, later to be given to the Museum as an invaluable nucleus, had been stimulated in 1913 by an exhibit in the New York Armory of the French Modernists, an exhibit held largely under the supervision of Arthur Davies, the American artist, who was himself perhaps the first to dream of a museum dedicated to the new and the revolutionary in art. Mrs. Sullivan, who had formerly been a teacher of art and who had long shared the dreams of Miss Bliss and Mr. Davies, was, with her husband, also a collector, but on a smaller scale than Miss

Bliss. Their hostess, as a purchaser of modern pictures, at this time lagged behind both her fellow conspirators; but her zeal for the non-conformist idea which they were about to submit to the unsuspecting Mr. Goodyear was as ardent as their own. Many conversations held by the three during the past years upon the regrettable state of modern art in New York City had prepared the way and set the stage for the exciting proposal which they had resolved to make to their guest from Buffalo.

To say that Mr. Goodyear was startled when he was asked to accept the chairmanship of a committee which should immediately organize a museum of modern art in New York is an understatement. He was so overcome that twenty-four hours in which to regain sufficient composure for reflection seemed essential to him. At the close of this interim, during which the three arbiters of his destiny breathlessly awaited his answer, he accepted with an eagerness approaching their own.

Things now moved with amazing rapidity. At Mr. Goodyear's suggestion, Mr. Frank Crowninshield, who as a friend of modern art had already published admirable reproductions of it in his magazine, *Vanity Fair*, joined the committee to contribute his urbanity, influence, and vitality, and occasionally to watch his ideas being demolished by the original three, whom he termed "the adamantine ladies." Within a few weeks two others of like minds had been added to it, Mrs. Murray Crane, who had drawn about her a circle of young people of advanced artistic interests, and Dr. Paul Sachs, Professor of Fine Arts at Harvard. These seven formed the original trustees of the new Museum, with Mr. Goodyear as its first president.

Even before the summer vacation of that extraordinary

year separated the promoters, the all-important problem of financial support was assured of solution, since over fifty persons professed themselves willing to contribute to this adventurous undertaking. Adequate quarters for the Museum were rented at 730 Fifth Avenue; in July an able young man, Alfred Barr, who was teaching art at Wellesley College, was appointed its director; and plans were well under way for its first exhibition to be held in November. When Mr. Goodyear sailed for Europe in August to obtain the loan of works of modern art for the opening of the new galleries, he had forgotten his initial shock of surprise in the whirlwind of activity in which he now found himself.

By October, seven additional trustees had been chosen from New York and elsewhere, all of whom were either collectors or persons prominent in various fields of artistic work. Abby Rockefeller was made the treasurer of this enlarged board, and a junior advisory committee was formed with her son Nelson as its chairman that the Museum might have the benefit of the fresh point of view of youth as well. From its ranks both trustees and staff members were later recruited who now play a leading role in the life of the Museum.

This was to be no magnificent mausoleum, no safe and silent repository for the work of artists already seriously established by time. Instead it was to be open to all new and significant developments in the world of art which modern life now offered and might more generously offer in the future, few of which developments had yet received serious attention from existing museums. Nor was it to be limited to what is commonly thought of as artistic creation, that is, to painting, sculpture, and drawing, alone. Although its aim was to encourage and to promote the study and the knowledge of modern art in terms of such creation, it proposed to widen and to apply such study to the material and the industrial world of its time. Even commercial art was not to be outside its limitless sphere. All its activities were, in short, to be interwoven with all aspects of modern life and to extend into literally every avenue of that life. Its foremost concern was with human beings, their practical needs as well as their possible artistic powers. Its goal was quite simply that of public service.

Not that all these aims were achieved at the start or all these activities put at once in motion even though they were recommended in the original "1929 Plan." Several of the trustees, themselves primarily interested in painting and sculpture, drawings and prints, did not at first approve the idea that the Museum should include a number of other arts outside these generally recognized fields. Some were frankly skeptical concerning the inclusion of industrial design, architecture, photography, and motion picture films. Abby Rockefeller, however, even though she was not herself particularly interested in movies, photography, and industrial design, recognized the great importance of these arts in modern life and their validity as a part of the program of the Museum. From the beginning she was whole-heartedly in favor of this broader project, which, backed by its enthusiastic supporters on the Board of Trustees and on the Museum Staff, advanced year by year toward fulfillment.

The first exhibition of the new Museum, held on November 7, 1929, and consisting largely of the work of nineteenth century French painters, won vast approval from the public. In one month it was seen by forty-seven thousand people, and relatively little adverse criticism of

135

its offerings was received. Such a halcyon atmosphere was not, however, to be generated by many later exhibits whether of the work of foreign or of American artists. The suspicion and resentment which Abby Rockefeller had foreseen before her prophetic luncheon party found frank and vehement expression. One critic took occasion to quote Dean Inge, who contended that anyone "intoxicated by the splendor of the Renaissance" must feel only horror at the revolting productions of the modernist school, which resemble "the work of a very unpleasant child, the first efforts of an African savage, or the hallucinations of an incurable lunatic." This critic continued with a suggestion of his own; namely, that the many fine insane asylums of the country might well be equipped with studios so that "their inmates might express themselves to their hearts' content."

Undeterred by such vituperation, since freedom of expression was one of its own ideals, the new Museum continued to fulfill its aims in terms of relationship with the public. In addition to its showings of painting and sculpture, it put forth exhibits of stage designs, scenery, and costumes, one of which covered five centuries of the art of the theatre and illustrated that art by work from fourteen countries; of architecture and government housing plans; of work sponsored by the Federal Art Project; of cave and rock paintings of prehistoric peoples; of bookbindings and household furniture; of photography and motion picture films; and a "Machine Art" exhibit, in which all the objects shown were produced by machines and which featured the best designs in practical articles from kitchen ware and lighting fixtures to gasoline pumps. Before three years had elapsed, it was beginning to send exhibitions of many sorts to other museums throughout the country in order not only to increase a knowledge and an appreciation of modern art, but to spread abroad the understanding that it was in no sense divorced from the concerns and necessities of daily living.

It is difficult to exaggerate the interest felt and the part played by Abby Aldrich Rockefeller in these early years of the Museum of Modern Art. Perhaps, outside her home, no other interest was quite comparable. Aside from many gifts of paintings, drawings, and sculpture from her steadily growing collection, quite apart from generous contributions of money and of land from both her and her husband which made possible its beautiful new building in 1939, she gave intangible offerings of greater value. Frankly, even hotly, protesting when she occasionally disapproved of a selection made for exhibits, but good-humored when her opinions were over-ridden; tolerant of extreme phases of art because of what they might conceivably say to others, if not to her; undismayed by carpings and criticism from the extreme right wing, yet always ready to battle for a principle; simple, unassuming, and forever gracious, she was, in truth, "the heart of the Museum, its center of gravity." By her outspoken courage, from which charm and humor were never absent, she could convince the doubtful just as by her abounding vitality she could lend new life to those who were depressed. In 1935, when certain trustees questioned the propriety and the relevance of a Film Library as well as its cost, she could persuade them that such an investment was neither mad nor impractical. At the close of a meeting during which a deplorably boring speaker had drained all good nature from his exhausted audience, she could retrieve ebbing courtesy by the quiet remark that she did not consider his reappearance an actual "necessity" and transmute irritation into amusement by her comment that such incredible dullness had, in fact, held an odd fascination for her since she had never before even imagined it to be possible.

From 1939, through crucial years when both the Museum staff and its Board of Trustees were depleted because of the war, she found time to give help and counsel to those who carried the responsibility for its work, especially to Mr. Stephen Clark, an early member of the Board, upon whose shoulders the main responsibility rested. That Mr. Clark valued her cooperation and assistance, he made clear in his description of their work together during this period.

In undertaking the management of the Museum during the war years, we were faced with an unusually difficult situation. Our chief concern was to try to keep the organization intact and to make the members of the staff work together in harmony. To accomplish that purpose we watched over the personnel with the most solicitous care and in some cases established a close and almost intimate personal relationship with members of the staff.

For both Mrs. Rockefeller and me this was a novel experience. Neither of us had ever seen at such close range the group of individuals who composed the staff of the Museum. Most of them were likable, extremely intelligent, and filled with a boundless enthusiasm for the Museum and all that it stood for. At the same time some were very temperamental in character, and there was occasionally bickering, jealousy, and dissension among them. Someone had to quiet their emotions, soothe their wounded feelings, and disengage them from violent controversies. In this field Mrs. Rockefeller had no equal. Everybody liked and admired her, and so great was her tact and understanding that, even when she had a disagreeable duty to perform, she left no scars behind. It was a constant source

of astonishment to me that she instinctively understood these people whose background and experience in life had been so different from her own.

Perhaps two of her contributions to the Museum and its aims deserve especial comment: her deep concern over its permanent Collection and her equally profound interest both in American art and in the work of living American artists. Of all the trustees she was one of the most devoted to its Collection. When certain members on the Board voted against using an unexpected gift for the addition of works of art, she privately gave money of her own. In 1938 she presented the Museum with its first large purchase fund, a sum generously increased by her son Nelson, who has been for many years President of the Museum and his mother's enthusiastic partner throughout. This fund has since been added to by other members of her family, and similar funds established by interested trustees, the largest by Mrs. Simon Guggenheim, one of the Museum's most ardent, generous and self-effacing supporters.

Although many of her associates on the Museum Board remained loyal in their private collections to the works of famous French masters, she gave staunch support to American artists. Not only did she buy their pictures, but she knew many of them personally, especially among the young, welcomed them to her home, and encouraged them in their work, never forgetting its value as American art whether or not she was personally enthusiastic over it. She did not always buy carefully, sometimes because she was eager to aid struggling and even hungry artists; but, though she occasionally made mistakes in terms of artistic value, she kept alive and growing a faith in the native

art of her own day, a faith which many young painters whom she knew and helped will remember.

She never forgot, or allowed others to forget, the idea and the principle which in the beginning had made possible the Museum, the vision which she constantly saw, that art, modern or ancient, has, above all else, a human value. Upon her death an editorial referred to her as "the most unconventional and effectual patron of art which America has seen." Recalling other pioneers far better known than herself, she would be the first to deny with laughter such an obvious overstatement. Yet she surely belongs among those in America and elsewhere who had visions of the wider horizons of art and who generously gave of their influence and imagination to make more certain its boundless contributions and resources to all men.

2

ON MAY 11, 1949, A LITTLE MORE THAN A YEAR AFTER HER death, the Abby Aldrich Rockefeller Print Room was formally opened at the Museum of Modern Art. This room had been designated by the trustees as a memorial to her, not only in recognition of her special interest in prints, but in grateful remembrance as well of her enthusiasm for the work of the Museum as a whole.

Two years before its founding she had begun to buy prints for her own collection, and by 1931 she was purchasing more, with the Museum in mind as the ultimate place in which they should be housed and preserved. Her interest in prints was a natural one. With her faith that art had many things to say to all manner of people, she

Mrs. Rockefeller with Grandchildren

was particularly inclined toward that form of it which might be easily available to all wanting good, yet inexpensive, pictures for their homes. Although her early purchases were largely those of the famous French modernists, Picasso, Degas, Gauguin and others, she became in later years strongly drawn toward the work of living Americans and bought extensively from their productions. When plans were being made in the late nineteen-thirties for the new Museum building, she argued for the inclusion of a print room, no matter what the cost of its equipment and upkeep. She won her argument, and space was set aside for such a room, the furnishing and opening of which were, however, because of the war, delayed for nine years.

In 1940 she gave to the Museum her collection of over sixteen hundred etchings, lithographs, and woodcuts to add to those which it had already received from Miss Bliss and other donors. At the close of the war she resumed her buying for the collection, and in 1946 presented some sixty valuable Lautrec lithographs. In the last weeks of her life she was eagerly looking forward to a personal exploration of the recent work of young American printmakers and planning to add from these also to the Museum collection.

Her tastes in art were definite, even unyielding. She knew precisely what she liked and did not like; and she was not easily persuaded to alter her judgments. The pictures and prints which she bought, first of all for herself, reflect her own inclinations and enjoyments. Yet whenever she gave a sum of money for the purchase of additions to the Museum galleries, she was careful to tie no strings whatever to her gift. When it left her bank account, it left also her surveillance.

Her tolerance and, at the same time, the integrity of her personal taste are illustrated by the acquisition of one of the most important works in her memorial print room, Picasso's impressive and formidable *Minotauromachy*, for which she felt neither affection nor admiration. She could not be persuaded to select it personally for the Museum; but with characteristic liberalism she gave the money for it, and then suggested with quick wit,

"Let's label this: *Purchased with a Fund for prints which Mrs. Rockefeller doesn't like.*"

3

DURING THE WAR YEARS THE MUSEUM, IN LINE WITH ITS principle of the indissoluble bond between life and art, undertook to cooperate with the Army's Special Services Division in its program for men in military camps throughout the country. Very early in the war the Division set up an art section, the purpose of which was to provide recreational activity for soldiers interested in art and to encourage them in the decoration of army camp buildings, especially in the painting of murals. Since the Special Services Division had few if any funds for free artists' materials, the Museum saw its opportunity and straightway formed its own Armed Services Program which determined to meet this need. Under the energetic direction of Mr. James Thrall Soby, who acted as Trustee Chairman of the Program, it began to look about for ways and means to accomplish its end. Through a sale of works of art, contributed by friends of the Museum, some $15,-000 was raised and used to supply necessary materials to army camps throughout the country. The Museum used also its prestige and influence to secure from army officers a greater interest in the work of really talented men who might otherwise have been overlooked or set at less congenial tasks. It likewise actively assisted the Red Cross in its arts and crafts program for men in military hospitals by securing teachers who could give them suitable instruction.

With some risk of desecration and damage to its premises it offered also during these years a variety of entertainments in its galleries and its garden. In the garden hundreds of men, American, British, and French, listened to music, enjoyed beer and sandwiches provided by a Salvation Army canteen installed there, and on one memorable summer night heard Gracie Fields sing to the accompaniment of their own roars of delighted applause. In the galleries occasional fist fights among soldiers and sailors and less serious altercations brought art close to life. Such disturbances were sometimes deeply resented by sightseers and students, at once more sober and more serious; but the trustees and the staff of the Museum remained undismayed.

These new and exciting projects and programs had no more eager supporter than Abby Rockefeller, to whom all such undertakings were in complete accordance with her original hope for the Museum; and early in 1944, when the war neared its close, she set forth upon yet another adventure, the idea of which was peculiarly her own. Encouraged by the success which had marked that earlier experiment in artistic expression among the fighting forces in camps and hospitals, she determined to found, in connection with the Museum, an organization to be known as the War Veterans' Art Center. Its goal was to be the re-

143

building, by means of the teaching and practice of art, of the minds and the outlooks of disabled men, the discovery within them of talents and resources heretofore either un-recognized or hindered by lack of opportunity for expression. With that drive characteristic of her once her mind was made up, that impatience of delay, she had by late spring chosen her helpers and with them decided upon the ways and means of carrying out her project. On June 12th of that same year her Center was ready to begin its work with a group of some eighteen disabled men.

Mr. Stephen Clark was her co-sponsor in this new enterprise; and Mr. Kenneth Chorley was named as chairman of the Committee which should direct the policy and the operation of the new Center. Throughout the four years of its life no chairman could have given more wise or enthusiastic cooperation.

A lively and eager young man, Victor D'Amico, who was on the staff of the Museum as director of art classes for children under its Educational Program, was chosen to supervise the activities of the Center. It became immediately apparent that no choice could have been a happier one. Mr. D'Amico was more than a brilliant and inspiring teacher. He cared for people, understood the mental and spiritual problems of men wounded not only in body but often in mind as well. They, on their part, liked and trusted him. He soon surrounded himself with a remarkable group of young and talented teachers whose enthusiasm and spirit of service were as deep as his own. "Mr. Clark and I merely supply the funds for the Center," his patroness and friend wrote her son David. "Nice Mr. D'Amico does all the work. He is a wonderful person. Every man loves and trusts him."

Mr. D'Amico felt himself equally fortunate. "Mrs.

144

Rockefeller was the mainspring of all we did," he said in recalling his work. "Her thinking went straight to the core of things. I never knew anyone who could go so quickly to the heart of a situation as she. She could not bear the idea of wasting time. She was always talking about using it, 'catching up with it' was her phrase. No man was just like any other fellow to her. He was always a man who could do something of his own that no one else could do as well; and it was her job as well as ours to find out what he could do and get him started on it."

In October, 1944, the War Veterans' Art Center moved to larger quarters, equipped with studios and shops, at 681 Fifth Avenue, where for four years it successfully carried out its purpose. Its program was extremely varied since it was governed by the specific needs and abilities of those who worked within it and who differed widely in aptitudes and inclinations. Careful effort was always made at the start to discover what each man could best do. Did his interest lie in drawing, painting, or sculpture, pottery, wood-carving, or book illustration, jewelry or metal work, or even in silk screen printing? Men were encouraged to explore a number of such fields until they found the one which best suited them.

Classes met in three-hour sessions for a period of three months on either one or two evenings a week. During this time the men in question not only discovered the work they could do best and liked most, but they received a foundation for pursuing it further, either professionally at some art school or as a hobby for odd, unemployed hours at home. Contrary to the view of many occupational therapists, good and careful craftsmanship was insisted upon from the start, just as the mere copying of designs and other methods of quick and easy success were discouraged on the ground that they would only prove deceptive in the end. In other words, since a genuine rebuilding of personality was the aim of the Center, an establishment of new confidence and security, honesty in all dealings was its groundwork.

In the second and third years of its life there was a constant waiting-list of eager applicants for its training. During the four years of its service it dealt with 1485 veterans, who represented all businesses, trades, and professions, from teaching, medicine, and dentistry to merchandising and stenography. Many of these men found abilities and talents within themselves sufficient to warrant a welcome change from former occupations; many found a means of greater financial security; practically all received new confidence and strength as well as fresh resources for the enjoyment and understanding of life.

In a letter written in 1945 its founder described a visit made to it.

After dinner I went to the Center to see it in operation. It was the first time I had been there actually to watch the men at work because Mr. D'Amico had thought that visitors might disturb them. Of course, you realize that all of them are men who have been wounded or who are suffering from the results of battle fatigue or shock. I don't think anyone would have realized the extent of some of their injuries except that some of them seemed frightfully nervous.

I thoroughly enjoyed walking about the rooms to see what they were doing. In the first room a group was working on jewelry. Most of them apparently had their minds set on modern design, but there were one or two young men who were more successful and ambitious. They were creating flowers in silver, such as women now wear on their coat lapels. In the middle room there was a class in painting. I saw no budding genius among them, but they were all deeply interested in what they were doing. At first they paid very little attention to me, but, as I wandered about, they began to talk to me and to explain just what they were trying to express and why they were doing it. In the next room men were working on the silk screen process. The first man I talked with was trying to reproduce some Marie Laurencin prints. I gathered that in this room they were doing this particular work because it might very much increase their ability to make a living.

We have great hopes for this work for all these men. And almost more encouraging than the work itself was the atmosphere of hope and confidence which I felt everywhere. That is just what art ought to give, and I came home very happy.

When the Center closed in June, 1948, because of the healthful decision that veterans ought no longer to be isolated from their fellow artists and craftsmen but should instead make their own destinies in the arts possible, a People's Art Center, open to all persons interested in forms of expression, took its place. This enlarged Center, operated under the Museum of Modern Art, now adds its contribution and meaning to the widespread activities of the Museum.

4

No UNDERTAKING OF ABBY ALDRICH ROCKEFELLER MORE clearly demonstrates her pride in America and in its cultural history than her collection of folk art which now hangs in the Ludwell-Paradise House in Colonial Williamsburg and which has deservedly won such enthusiastic admiration both at home and abroad. From 1931, when

147

she first began to acquire American folk paintings, until,
in 1939, she presented her entire collection to Williamsburg,[1] she was employing every means to discover and to
preserve these evidences of our native art of the late eight-
eenth century and the first half of the nineteenth. The
collection is both a record of American life in terms of its
artistic expression and an authentic document of that life
as it was lived before the industrial age.

It records those years in American history when, after
the baffling problems of a new world had been solved by
the colonists and after the War of the Revolution had
finally shattered an earlier dependence upon the culture
and learning of England, a new American people began
for the first time to stand alone, to work out its own destiny as a nation. An era of relative prosperity, which
followed the disturbance of war, and a more leisurely
existence than had been possible in years of settlement
were conducive to the development of art. Those many
female seminaries, which sprang up everywhere in the
early nineteenth century, added their encouragement also;
for young ladies, who in an earlier century had expressed
themselves in needlework, were taught now drawing and
painting for the decoration of their future homes. In their
more doleful hours, they created "mourning pictures" of
dismal and sorrowing groups with handkerchiefs pressed
to their streaming eyes. Sometimes the growth of this native art developed from humbler occupations. A house
painter might feel a desire to paint portraits of his family
or his neighbors or to transfer to canvas his pleasure in

[1] To the Museum of Modern Art she gave certain fine examples of
this folk art which were later bought by the Metropolitan Museum under
a reciprocal agreement.

the landscape seen from his home, and, delighted with his newly discovered talent, continue with it in his leisure time. Itinerant painters, who wandered about the country-side in search of a living, found use for their paints and brushes through that human desire for even a brief immortality latent in the minds of those whom they called upon in hope.

This American folk art at Williamsburg, which is preserved in one of the most beautiful of the restored houses there, represents work in oils, watercolors, and pastels, as well as in odd pen drawings, paintings on velvet and on glass, needlework, and sculptures in wood and metal. Gathered from twenty states of the Union, these present a cross section of the art produced in our country by little known or anonymous craftsmen and artists. Its charm and humor delight all who see it as they never failed to delight its collector and donor, who during her frequent stays at Williamsburg loved to look at it and to give privately conceived names to certain especially appealing portraits.

In securing her folk art she did not depend upon dealers alone although she often bought from them. Instead she made every effort to find pictures and sculpture on their native soil. In this task she was greatly assisted by Mr. Holger Cahill, the principal authority on American folk art, who acted as her agent in discovering many of the best things in her collection. Travelling through many states, particularly those of the South, he brought to light from attics and sitting-rooms, carpenters' shops and forges, many of the creations now shown at Williamsburg and learned as much as possible concerning their origin. His knowledge and enthusiasm, together with his discovery and evaluation of pictures in their own settings, have given to the collection a scope and a quality unequalled elsewhere.

The folk art in the Ludwell-Paradise House gives the beholder an extraordinary and lasting impression difficult to describe. Although the paintings merely as paintings are sometimes amateurish and even crude, they emanate an honesty and integrity not soon forgotten. One comes suddenly to the realization that here are the fresh and original aspirations of a people, who, from New England and the Pennsylvania German settlements, from Ohio and the South, have placed on canvas, or wood, or metal, not only the character and quality of their own imaginations, but as well the spirit of a country.

5

THERE WAS YET ANOTHER FOLK ART AT WILLIAMSBURG OF which Abby Rockefeller was herself the creator and for which, during the springs and autumns of many years, she worked devotedly. Concerned as she had been throughout her life with the welfare of minority groups, she was especially interested in the better living conditions and in the education of the colored people of the Williamsburg area. In 1942 she contributed a large sum of money toward a school and community center for the negroes there.

One of them expressed, for all, their gratitude both for her gift and for her friendliness when he said:

"There is a new future for my people here at Williamsburg because of our school at Bruton Heights. But Mrs. Rockefeller gave us something more than money. She made us feel a part of the community and even a part of her own life. Every one of us has wanted to be a better citizen just because of what she was here in all these years.

"I would not dare to call myself a good man, but every man wanted to be good when he was with her."

EIGHT

FULFILLMENT

ALL HER LIFE ABBY ROCKEFELLER FOUND RESTING DIFFI-
cult to plan for and irksome to endure. "I suppose I must
hurry up and rest," she used to say to her New York housekeeper. "I have a wonderful new doctor," she wrote one
of her sons. "He's very skillful, but I love him mostly because he doesn't bother me much, except for telling me to
rest far more than I do." She was not given to worrying
over the state of her earthly tabernacle; and none of her
family ever heard her complain over ills of the flesh, although for some years her heart, in physical terms, had
not been in the best condition. This, though recognized,
had never caused her undue anxiety since she had far more
important matters to think about. In the last few years of
her life, however, her health began to claim more consideration; and in the winters of 1947 and 1948 she spent two
months in Arizona with her husband. There she found
that resting was not, after all, so disagreeable an occupation.

She loved the deserts and mountains of the Southwest
and took unceasing delight in the open stretches of country, the changing clouds, the brilliant colors of sky and
land. She adored the almost constant sunshine. "I never
before have quite realized what the sun can do for one.
Now I can understand better why there were ancient sun-
worshippers. I'm almost one myself." In the bright sun-
light of the patio of their small cottage, attached to the
inn at Tucson, she sat for hours under a pepper tree, which

she described in many of her letters since she never tired of its beauty. She loved watching the birds and scaring away the cats, too numerous because a tender-hearted neighbor was given to feeding them. Needlepoint kept her hands busy while she dictated letters to her family.

On many days she and her husband drove into the desert or to the mountains for a picnic lunch. Once they had found a place which seemed perfect to them both, they set up two folding chairs and the box which served them as a table. Then they gathered some twigs and bits of wood for their fire and toasted their sandwiches on forked sticks or on a hot-dog roaster. Coffee in a thermos bottle, a little fruit, and a piece of cake, which he easily resisted, but which she never could forego, completed their repast but not their pleasure. After lunch was over, they searched for desert or mountain flowers, often the delicate and unfamiliar blossoms of different varieties of the cactus. These she placed in a jar filled with water and always brought along for that purpose. Later she could study and identify them in their sitting-room.

Long, quiet evenings were devoted to reading. Her husband read aloud to her while she worked on tapestry for him and for her daughters-in-law. They both enjoyed the re-reading of *Jane Eyre*, a favorite of years ago, but *Wuthering Heights*, to her amusement, made him "creepy"; in fact, he quite frankly "detested" those wild happenings on the Yorkshire moors. Others among the English novelists made these evenings memorable in that rare companionship which they had known over many years. Friends also, coming from here and there, added to their pleasure, especially since her husband possessed a happy genius for terminating with perfect courtesy all such social occasions at just the right moment.

156

There was always Williamsburg to look forward to, once they had returned home in April. She loved the spring in Virginia. The small white house, known as Bassett Hall and set well back from the main road beyond its own avenue of elms and ailanthus trees, was in its size, age, and simplicity especially dear to her. Its garden which she had helped to make; the thousands of daffodils which would be in bloom under the trees; the shining leaves of the holly and the distorted, interwoven, rust-colored branches of the old mulberries; the great oaks that stood about on the long reaches of green and open land; the cardinals, mocking birds, and thrushes which perched on her feeding-boxes just beyond the stone terrace; the woods in the distance where they loved to walk; her neighbors ready to welcome her home—these she always anticipated with pleasure.

In 1948 there was no return to Williamsburg. They came back to New York early in April, rested and refreshed by their stay in Arizona. Eager to see her children and grandchildren, she had planned a family reunion at Pocantico Hills and went there almost immediately upon their arrival home.

During the drive from New York to Pocantico on the first Friday afternoon in April, she talked with her son Nelson about art in America, speaking excitedly of a new recognition of it, a new understanding of its place in our life. She felt sure that it was at last coming to maturity, that here as in Paris people would be sitting around tables in the garden of the Museum, talking as they had always talked in Europe of the work of many artists, avidly discussing new exhibitions, values of this picture and that, the meaning behind techniques, designs, colors, what these were saying to persons of every sort. She was eager to re-

157

sume her activities at the Museum, to get in touch with some young American print-makers of whom she had heard, to discover and encourage new talent.

The two days at Pocantico were, she said, the happiest she had ever known. Her violets, her red and white trilliums were pushing aside the soil along the garden walks; her red hawthorns, her lilacs, and fruit trees were clothed in a mist of new green; the forsythia was bursting into bloom; baby ducks were busy about the lake; baby geese were waddling importantly after their parents over the new grass. The house was filled with spring flowers to celebrate her home-coming. Everything, herself included, was new and young.

Many of her family spent the two days with her, grandchildren running about the house and garden, eating luncheon with her, telling her of all that had happened since she had last seen them. One little boy had Sunday breakfast with her alone in her sitting-room. There were laughter and merriment during those two days, and everywhere a sense of spring.

On Sunday afternoon, before she drove back to New York with her son David, she insisted upon putting on a new dress and hat. "I've got to wear something entirely new," she said, "for I've never been so happy in all my life!" She held her newest grandchild on her lap all the way home; and, once there, still overflowing with the joy of her return, she went to see a son's new home, his rugs which she wanted to pass judgment on, his new walls and pictures. Nor would she be deterred from visiting her most recent daughter-in-law, whom she had not been able to welcome except by letter, since her marriage. She could not bear the day to end, she told her husband; and before she went to bed, she telephoned to her sister Lucy in Providence to say that, with her family about her, she had had the most wonderful time in all her seventy-four years.

It was a day of fulfillment and her last on this earth. She died early the next morning, the 5th of April, 1948.